YOU AND VALUES EDUCATION

YOU AND VALUES
EDUCATION

Charles R. Kniker

Iowa State University

CHARLES E. MERRILL PUBLISHING COMPANY
A Bell & Howell Company
Columbus, Ohio

125120

to

Eleanor   *Ted*   *Tim*

. . . special beyond words

Published by
CHARLES E. MERRILL PUBLISHING COMPANY
A Bell & Howell Company
Columbus, Ohio 43216

This book was set in Palatino and Optima.
The production editor was Frances Margolin.
The cover was designed by Will Chenoweth.

International Standard Book Number: 0-675-08516-0

Library of Congress Catalog Number: 76-26356

1 2 3 4 5 6 81 80 79 78 77

Printed in the United States of America

Preface

Education, at its best, promotes a continuous search for truth and a commitment to improve instruction. At its worst, education encourages impatience and the use of jargon in its attempts at reform.

The movement toward values education is a prime example. For some it is an old program—character education, updated. For others it is the effort to regain a balance between cognitive and affective instruction. Certain advocates see it as the key to humanizing education. Some critics view it as a series of techniques to entertain students, or worse, a clever system to indoctrinate learners. Bewildered citizens and harried teachers may feel this is just one more responsibility the schools are to accept since other institutions are failing to carry out their functions.

Unlike many other books in this field, which promote only one dimension of values education, this book will examine the variety of approaches now available to teachers. The reader will be able to put values education in perspective, historically and philosophically; the reader will learn about the large number of curricular and nonprint materials now available; and the reader will receive suggestions on how to "customize" values activities for his or her own situation.

The book is written primarily for educators, those preparing to be teachers, and those who are instructors. However, it is written broadly enough to be of interest to those in religious work, civic clubs, and youth agencies.

Most likely *You and Values Education* will be adopted as a text or supplementary material for a general education methods course. Since many of the activities come from practicing teachers, it is also appropriate as a reference for inservice workshops and school libraries for faculty. It could also be a helpful aid in an introduction to education class if the students are exploring their attitudes about teaching as a career. Issues in education courses which examine the values education movement may find this book provides useful background information.

Finally, note that the book is written in a personal and active style. It is designed to help the reader ask, "What are my values?" and "If I teach, how will I approach value questions?" To help answer these questions, the book provides a number of values activities which reflect several approaches currently being used as well as introduce the reader to a variety of new activities which have been developed by me and my students.

Acknowledgements

Many individuals have been instrumental in the shaping of this book. I am indebted to them for producing this "return" from a small investment begun six years ago.

The College of Education, Iowa State University, has both provided an environment for and the encouragement to explore values education. Specifically I wish to thank Virgil S. Lagomarcino, Dean of the College; Harold E. Dilts, Associate Dean and department head, secondary education; and Ray Bryan, former department head, professional studies. Colleagues Dominick D. Pellegreno, Donald G. Zytowski, Fred G. Brown, and Michael Simonson made helpful comments on portions of the manuscript.

Douglas Superka, Social Science Education Consortium, Boulder, Colorado, graciously consented to let me adapt his typology of approaches and offered many meaningful suggestions. Roberta Atwell, Grinnell College, and Virginia Hash, University of Northern Iowa, provided valuable ideas.

For the students at Creston, Council Bluffs, Audubon, Spencer, and Mason City, as well as Ames, who shared value strategies and contributed their activities, I shall always have gratitude and warm memories.

As the manuscript neared completion, two students became deeply involved in providing assistance. Nancy Tucker Morris has displayed remarkable talent as an idea clarifier and proof reader. Phil Murrell has given generously of his time to provide ideas for illustrations which give life to the concepts expressed in the book.

This total project would not have succeeded had it not been for the continued interest of Tom Hutchinson, college education editor at Charles E. Merrill.

Contents

125120

Appendixes

Indexes

INTRODUCTION

You and Values Education

The title of this book has been carefully chosen to reflect three major points which I want to make.

"You" begins the title because I believe you, and others like you who are concerned about values education, are much more important than the myriad techniques or curriculum sets which are supposed to bring about dramatic changes in students' value systems. The success of any values program—whether carried on in schools, colleges and universities, religious agencies, or civic groups—will depend more on the attitudes and values held by the participants, leaders, and learners than upon the materials they choose to use.

That noted, the title further implies that you have some *choices* when it comes to selecting which approach or approaches to values education are most appropriate for your educational situation. Unlike some books in this field, which only describe one perspective for values instruction, this book presents a variety of methods. You can choose the ones which compliment your personal teaching style and, if need be, are consistent with the policies of the educational agency with which you work. For me to insist that there is only one way to approach values education would be to inflict *my* value preferences upon you.

Yet I have to add, and this is my third point, that I *do* have some assumptions about what makes values education most effective. In my earlier drafts I wanted to be nondirective; I deliberately down-played those techniques which I favored so that each reader could select his or her favorite approach without pressure. Reviewers and students urged me to include the approach to values education which has proved most successful for me. I call it *values investment* because I believe that values education is most effective when it requires learners to invest something of themselves, both in discussions about value positions and in actual demonstrations of their values. My approach uses systematically planned activities that require participants to invest their time, talents, energies, money, and reputation. But it goes beyond just doing the activities. Meaningful evaluation techniques are also suggested. But more about values investment later.

In summary, this book is directed to you if you are concerned about the development of values in the educational process. You may be an undergraduate planning a teaching career or a practicing teacher. You may be a youth worker, adult educator coordinator, or a religious educator. Perhaps you are not a professional educator, but a parent or school patron concerned about a values curriculum your school districts plans to adopt.

I cannot stress enough that this book is for you to adapt as much as possible. Join me now for a treasure hunt through the riches of values education. Let's hope that you uncover and develop values activities that "yield" great dividends.

LOOKING AHEAD

The values investment approach I just described has also influenced the way I constructed this book. Generally speaking, an investment is a commitment of your resources, through the services of a broker or manager, for the purpose of gaining a favorable return. There are significant parallels between the investment process and the other values education approaches being advocated today.

Typically, there are three steps in making an investment. First, you examine a *prospectus.* A prospectus is a preliminary statement of an enterprise, stating existing conditions and giving basic information. It is calculated to arouse interest and win support for the program. In this book chapters 1 and 2 constitute the prospectus. The first chapter, "Developing Values Education," discusses briefly such historical and philosophical questions as: Can values be taught? What have schools been expected to do about values education? How can teachers approach values instruction? The values investment approach will describe the teacher's role as similar to that of the investment manager or broker. Chapter 2 focuses on evidence from psychologists and educational theorists on how people learn their values. The heart of the chapter is devoted to the description of nine possible ways to approach values education.

Second, if you wish to make an investment, you will probably want to see the investment manager's *portfolio*. In the world of finance, the portfolio contains descriptions of stocks and bonds which the manager feels are worthy investments. The portfolio of the values education field are the resources available to help raise values issues. Chapter 3, "Surveying Values Curriculum," is a survey of the formal curriculum sets now available, and the books related to the nine approaches. The strengths and weaknesses of various materials are discussed. Chapter 4, "Viewing Values Media," provides a rationale for using media in the affective domain, cites general reference works, and suggests some specific instructional media which may be beneficial. Descriptions of such media as films and filmstrips, television series, simulations and educational games, and independent projects are included.

Third, if you are seeking to make an investment, you would plan for your *return*, or "payoff." The last three chapters of the book focus on the planning of values education for individual situations. Typically all of us find that we must improvise from time to time. These three chapters should help you "customize" or individualize value strategies for your particular circumstances. In chapter 5, "Designing Value Objectives," you are given suggestions on how to better formulate objectives in the affective domain. "Assessing Value Positions," chapter 6, concentrates on techniques, from standardized tests to observation methods to role playing, which can help you and your students assess your "returns." Chapter 7, "Constructing Value Activities," details ways by which you can apply the values investment approach inexpensively! This chapter was written at the request of many teachers who could not afford to purchase curriculum sets. It includes a number of activities which my students developed.

THE VALUES INVESTMENT APPROACH

The word *value* has already appeared frequently in this book. Just what *is* a value? you may ask. I define a value as **a cluster of attitudes which generates either an action or a decision to deliberately avoid an action.**

Values are thus integral parts of the human experience. All of us have attitudes about other individuals in society, from political leaders to sports heroes to neighborhood merchants to members of our families.

These attitudes are constantly being refined. They result in values systems which, in turn, produce behavior patterns in our lives that may be constructive or destructive.

Because values are such a basic part of life, I believe they cannot be ignored in educational settings. But how should values questions be treated?

People who take the values investment approach assume that such an important dimension of life must be explored systematically. We further assume that the widest range of activities must be employed. Some will be cognitive—perhaps questionnaires, continuums, diaries, or analyses of moral dilemmas. Others will be affective—they will ask participants to share their feelings about a film or painting, or to construct a model, or to engage in a simulation. The blend of these activities will always move toward eventual expression of the learners' values.

More specifically, if you are a leader or a prospective leader of an educational group, the values investment approach would expect you to:

1.   Appraise your personal value system.

2.   Assess realistically what value goals you (and possibly your sponsoring educational agency) have in mind for students. Is it to indoctrinate children with the "right" values? Is it to expand their abilities to express their emotions more freely?

3.   Evaluate what teaching methods work best for you and your group.

4.   Choose those types of value activities which blend items **1** through **3.**

5.   Allow enough time to permit full discussion of student opinions, including reactions to the advantages, risks, and consequences of the strategies you use.

6.   Commit yourself and your learners to deadlines by which you will have sufficient opportunities to have expressed your value decisions through appropriate actions.

7.   Weigh with your group the return or payoff from having done the value strategies.

When I outline planned value strategies in the manner illustrated below, later I can judge better which ones were of most benefit to my students. Note the acronym **V-A-L-U-E-S.**

The Ⓥalue identification is the name of the activity. Sometimes I add a statement which summarizes the action the group will do.

The Activity states in behavioral terms the value topic to be engaged in and the change the participant will undergo.

The Learning aids section states what materials will be needed. You can jot down in this space the sources of films or stories used.

The Unit interaction details the activity, including the time needed and the age levels with which this strategy works. You can amplify it as much as you wish. You may write down that you will show a filmstrip and use the questions provided in the guidebook that accompanied the strip. Or you may prefer to outline the procedure you wish the class to follow.

The Evaluation segment lists the instruments you will use to find out what impact the strategy had upon the group. Will you use a self-report, a creative project, a letter to the editor, or a questionnaire? If you indicate class discussion will be the best technique for assessing the affective outcome, you may wish to write down the discussion questions in this section.

The Suggestions category is used to make notes to yourself for the future. You may find that a role play included characters to whom your students could not relate. If someone in your class raised a good question, you could note it here for the next time you do the activity.

Throughout the book I provide value activities to involve you with values education. Usually the activity will begin with the general instructions I would give you if I were with you or your group. Following each activity is an analysis of what I intended the strategy to accomplish. As you will see in chapter 7 when I cite strategies developed by teachers with whom I have worked, it is not necessary that you follow the V-A-L-U-E-S outline slavishly. As part of the explanation of each values activity, I attempt to indicate with what groups the strategy works well.

A SAMPLE ACTIVITY

Let's imagine that we are part of a group meeting for the first time. To get acquainted let's make a name tag—but not the traditional kind which only lists your name and the agency you represent. On a card or piece of paper write the name you like to be called. Then, as the illustration indicates, picture your favorite hobby, a place you'd like to visit, and a special event that either will take place in the next year or that has taken place in the last three months. Your card might look like Figure I-1.

Figure I–1

If we were in a group, I would have the group circulate after completing the name tags and then have discussion. Here's how I would structure the activity and evaluate it using the **V-A-L-U-E-S** acronym.

Value identification: "Name Tag."

Activity: After constructing name tags, participants compare and contrast the different preferences of the individuals present.

Learning aids: **1.** 5" X 8" cards, or pieces of construction paper.
   2.   Magic markers or coloring pencils, pieces of colored papers, scissors, and glue.
   3.   Straight pins or string.

Unit interaction: Junior-High-Adult. Spend fifteen to twenty minutes allowing the group to create symbols of their interests and events. Urge them to use symbols and avoid words. Decide whether or not you believe it is best to avoid job-related categories.

After tags are completed, participants should meet each other. After sufficient time for sharing their name tags has passed, have the group discuss what they found.

Evaluation: Group discussion. Possible questions:

1. Were you surprised by the choices of others in the group whom you knew previously?

2. Were you surprised by the choices made by those whom you had just met?

3. Could you guess much about the background of others, based on their symbols?

4. Was there much difference in the colors used to describe individual interests?

At the end of the evening or at the beginning of the next meeting, you might ask everyone to recall one of the symbols on another person's card.

Suggestions: Variations of this activity include an "-ing" name tag and a "fact" name tag. The participants list four qualities about themselves, such as "I'm lov*ing,* griev*ing,* bak*ing* . . ." or "I'm forty-four years old, the father of three children, a veteran of . . .". These strategies were developed by Sidney Simon. You might try a "guess who" name tag. Each person develops his or her tag secretly. The leader collects them and sees if the group can guess the originators.

SUMMARY

Unlike some recent books in the field of values education which tend to be "cookbooks," i.e., lists of strategies or recipes, this book provides a theoretical basis from which you can develop your own approach to values education. In some respects this book is like the nineteenth-century McGuffey's *Eclectic Readers,* for it compiles a variety of techniques and approaches with which to treat affective learning.

Although I offer an approach which I have found successful, I am not so much concerned that you adopt my model as that you become more aware of the many ways you might become a better values educator.

part one

THE
PROSPECTUS

The Prospectus *presents the historical and philosophical rationale for values educa-tion.*

Chapter 1 argues that the educational enterprise always has been and is likely to remain as much concerned about value issues as it is about cognitive skills. The key question for you to answer is "What kind of a values educator will I be?" rather than "Should I be a values educator?"

Chapter 2 focuses on the problems of defining values and distinguishing them from attitudes and beliefs. Some attention is given to the evidence on how people change their values. The basic decision you will be concerned with in this chapter is "Which of the nine approaches to values education is most closely related to my personal and philosoph-ical beliefs about teaching?"

Developing
Values Education

Values education has clearly arrived. The term *values education* serves as an umbrella for a number of efforts which want schools to give more attention to students' values, attitudes, and feelings. These approaches include character education, values clarification, moral development, motivation achievement, confluent education, a curriculum of affect, humanistic education, and transactional analysis.

Professional educator groups, such as the National Education Association and the American Society for Curriculum Development, have issued yearbooks and study guides on values education. Various state legislatures have mandated the study of "moral and spiritual values." Some states now require that prospective teachers have "human relations" components in their undergraduate studies.[1]

This chapter demonstrates that this interest in values education, and the objections to it, is not really a new phenomenon. The major sections of the chapter are the objections to values education, arguments in favor of values education, and development of *your* approach to values education. Each section contains at least one values activity. The chapter closes with two values activities, one for elementary and one for secondary students.

OBJECTIONS TO VALUES EDUCATION

Not everyone is happy with the movement toward a more formal approach to values education. One often-heard objection is that the primary task of schools is to teach basic skills (the three r's), or useful knowledge. It is argued that this cognitive competence prepares children to be productive workers in our technological society. Considering the limited time and resources schools have, as well as their charge from society to produce contributing members of the culture, the schools must concentrate upon "academic" subjects.

Others argue that the fundamental purpose of the public school system is to transmit a common curriculum along with a select number of experiences which will result in literate citizens, committed to a democratic lifestyle. R. Freeman Butts, an historian of education at Teachers College, Columbia University, has labeled this the "sense of belonging," which is the great idea of American education.[2] To do more than this, for instance, to allow for a comprehensive review of the numerous ethnic and personal value systems in this country, would defeat the purpose of a common school philosophy.

Still others believe that it is impossible or useless for teachers to attempt to "teach" values. Some say that it is the responsibility of other agencies, primarily the home and religious institutions. Legally, they could add, on the related matter of teaching religion in the schools, the United States Supreme Court has ruled that the official stance of the schools must be neutral. They could cite numerous cases where teachers who were to teach objectively about religions instead indoctrinated their students.[3] They feel that, despite good intentions, values education will soon slide into the realm of ethical manipulation. Others would cite psychological evidence indicating that values are formulated by the time children enter school and that attempts to "improve" or clarify values are ineffectual.

For an excellent review of the pros and cons of values education, see the June, 1975, *Phi Delta Kappan* and the October, 1975, issue of *Learning.*[4]

In light of the comments just made, write down what you believe the major goal of the American public school system should be.

If your statement emphasizes basic skills or vocational training, what do you think the school's role should be regarding students' personal or social values?

Keep these statements. When you finish the book refer to them again. See if your point of view has changed.

SCHOOLS ARE IN THE VALUES BUSINESS

Once when I was addressing a parent–teacher organization on the topic of values education, a member of the audience insisted that "schools should not be in the values business." The speaker made a number of objections to values education. I responded then, and still do, that schools *should* be in the values business; and as the evidence, historical and psychological, will show, they always have been.

An Historical Review

From the Puritan plantations to the Playboy and Playgirl era of today, the American schools have always been expected to deal with values. Quickly, let's look at the goals and typical graduates of major periods in our history.[5]

In colonial New England, the earliest laws requiring communities to provide schools did so because they believed that students who could read (the Bible, primarily) would be able to resist "ye old deluder Satan."

The educational objectives of Spanish missions dotting the Southwest and Far West were similar. The alien culture outside and the closeness of compound living made teaching the "true faith" fundamental.

In the southern colonies, private tutoring was the dominant teaching style but the goals again were not dissimilar. The curriculum emphasized business skills for the future plantation owner and social graces for the mistress of the house. But instructions in these "practical" duties were tempered by texts such as Baily's *Practice of Piety,* which laid out a schedule of devotional responsibilities for persons of standing, and *The Complet Gentleman* [sic], an etiquette manual which listed the ethical obligations of the privileged.

In the middle colonies, where European emigrants rubbed shoulders with the native Americans, the new citizens were forced to live with paradoxical goals. Denominational schools and private academies tried to retain the religious and lingual traditions of the old world. But they were gradually nudged into forging new lifestyles more compatible with the new surroundings.

Regardless of geographical location, then, the schools were committed to producing graduates who would be *literate saints.* Their textbooks were filled with biblical imagery; their leisure reading materials, such as almanacs, were freighted with moral stories (a favorite theme was that virtue is rewarded and vice is punished).[6]

During the early years of the republic, roughly from the time of the Revolutionary War to the eve of the Civil War, the nation reordered the priorities of schooling. To many of the country's founders, the fledgling nation was a "great experiment," even a second Zion. This spirit was to be adopted by early educational statesmen, who saw the schools as the training ground for loyal Americans and humanitarian reformers. Graduates were *loyal craftsmen.* Horace Mann, called *the father of the common school,* commented:

> Our means of education are the grand machinery by which the "raw material" of human nature can be worked up into inventors and

discoverers, into skilled artisans and scientific farmers, into scholars and jurists, into the founders of benevolent institutions, and the great expounders of ethical and theological science.[7]

After the guns were still at Appomattox, the westward movement exploded in America. The western geographical frontier was only one of many frontiers. New frontiers were conquered in technology (telegraph, electric lights), in economics (the trusts), and in education (the large systems in urban centers trying to educate immigrants). The frontier was characterized by the "railroad mentality." Such virtues as punctuality, hard work, honesty, competition (interpreted as "survival of the fittest"), and thrift became more predominant in the school literature. Increasingly, the public schools were expected to turn out graduates who would become *compliant clerks*—or, if they failed, menial workers.

As the twentieth century began, modifications were made in the American schools. More and more people moved to urban areas. The first world war and the Great Depression stunned the nation . Educators were asked to halt the moral drift which had begun following the war.

The most imposing educational document of this period was a report issued in 1918 by a National Educational Association Commission, which called for high schools to review and reform their curricula to meet "seven cardinal principles." Heading the list of values was health. Also included were "worthy home membership, citizenship, worthy use of leisure, and ethical character."[8] Evidently, the reform efforts were not sufficient; and in the 1940s a second movement calling for "life-adjustment education" flowered.[9]

Life adjustment was a precursor of career education, in that it sought to prepare youths for meaningful employment. This innovation apparently didn't satisfy the wishes of educational leaders for more affective education. The mid-fifties saw another NEA Commission issue a report titled "Moral and Spiritual Values in the Public Schools."[10] It concluded that a prime function of the schools was to transmit certain basic values, the primary one being the belief that "the individual was of supreme importance." Many of the other values listed—brotherhood, the pursuit of happiness, devotion to truth—supported the commission's statement that technological solutions were not ultimate answers. In short, graduates were *contented citizens.*

Goaded by the flight of Sputnik in 1957 and the frictions of the cold war, America shelved its "moral and spiritual values" programs. The push was on for graduates who were more than contented citizens. The nation wanted individuals who were both technically competent in some specialty and yet highly flexible in lifestyle (especially in moving about the country).

In the mid-1960s , when the space race was being run in earnest and the Vietnam War was producing its many lights at the end of the tunnel, the human potential movement emerged.[11] This was a time of discontent, and critics of the schools emerged. One very famous critic was A. S. Neill of Summerhill.[12] It is quite understandable that programs related to values education, such as black studies, ethnic heritage programs, and sex and drug education, were developed.

What kind of graduate is the school expected to produce in the late 1970s? In theory, at least, it appears that we want an *explorer*—someone grounded in a solid academic program, vocationally bent, who is also flexible enough to adjust to a rapidly changing future.

In summary, in every period Americans have asked the schools to transmit what they consider to be critical values for the survival of the community and nation. And it seems unlikely that society will stop asking the schools to transmit values.

Interestingly, a review of the major national statements calling for programs of moral education indicates that such pronouncements usually occurred within a decade after a war. Further, whenever the nation is perceived to be facing a monumental crisis, external or internal, the schools are asked to solve the problem. Given such tremendous tasks, it's surprising that schools have not buckled under more often than they have. As it is, schools have been aptly labeled "the imperfect panacea."

Clearly, schools have been and will continue to be in the value business.

The Psychological Structure of Schools

Historical precedents are not always convincing. We can say, and rightly so, that because it has been that way before does not guarantee it will be that way tomorrow. But those who argue that the schools are not in the values business must face the physical and psychological structures the schools do have.

The fact that society requires students to attend so many days per year and so many years tells the students something about the nation's values. In addition, the way students' time is regulated inside the building is another tip-off. (How many minutes must you take mathematics? What does the state require in physical education?)

In addition to the time structure, the building structure itself is a dead giveaway about the community's values. Does the building give you feelings of warmth, excitement, wanting to explore, or does it say this is an adult world, a prison, a mortuary? Are the hallways "clean as a whistle" with only properly authorized signs posted, or are they plastered with student art work and a bit untidy? What kind of facilities

This one was awarded by the taxpayers association!

does the science department have? Art or music? Is there a trophy case in the lobby? If so, what's in it?

The values promoted in schools surface in dress and hair codes and in posted signs. Of course, schools, and other institutions for that matter, also have unwritten policies. If you scan student and teacher handbooks, you can soon draw up extensive lists of "unforgiveable" and "tolerable, but frowned on" behaviors.

Within the classroom the student is confronted with another facet of the society's value structure, the teacher. We assume that not just anyone can become a teacher. Increasingly, school districts are turning to more sophisticated tools to interview prospective teachers. Some districts employ consulting firms which evaluate teacher candidates through tape-recorded interviews. In many communities, teachers are still expected to be models of propriety and, in turn, are to mold student lives.

The curriculum is another indicator of what is considered desirable to learn. Teachers cannot possibly present all materials or points of view, so their selection of what to present reflects their value judgments. The textbooks used represent the values of either a local teacher–administrator committee, a parent's group, or a state textbook committee. Textbook censorship controversies continue to erupt when parents feel strongly that schools are not promoting the "right" values.

Even in the extracurricular activities sponsored by the school we see the signposts of values. How important is athletics? Who gets to be editor of the school newspaper?

In short, try as you will, the psychological structure of the school places any teacher in the role of a values transmitter. To resist teaching certain values indicates that you are advocating certain other standards. To pretend that you can avoid values in the schools is to ignore reality, as John Holt and this cartoon suggest.[13]

Dick & Jane

Do you remember Dick and Jane?
See how they look now.
"Things certainly have changed," said Dick.
"They certainly have," said Jane.
Change, change, change.

Used by permission of United Church Press.

Value Activity: "Publish or Perish"

Examine some old school textbooks. You can easily obtain modern facsimilies of such old standards as the *Hornbook,* the *New England Primer,* and *McGuffey's Readers.* Don't forget to look at a "Dick and Jane" text. Obviously, include textbooks that are current, too.

First, find a value message in each book. Do schools today still promote these values (through the variety of ways mentioned above)?

What kind of people do you think write school textbooks? How are minority groups (political, racial, economic, religious) treated? What stereotypes about families and the roles of males and females are shown?

Pretend that you are an editor in a publishing company. If you were to select a manuscript for publication, what would you want it to stress? Is there some issue you feel is vital for all students to discuss?

Value identification: "Publish or Perish."

Activity: After each participant locates a value message in an old textbook, he or she explains why the society of that period tried to transmit the described value. If time permits, participants might be asked to identify a value they believe ought to be transmitted through textbooks today.

Learning aids: **1.** A collection of older textbooks. Modern reprints of old classics are available, such as the *Hornbook,* from the Hornbook, Inc., 585 Boylston St., Boston, *New England Primer* from Teachers College Press, New York, and *McGuffey's Fifth Reader,* from Signet Classics of the New American Library, New York.

2. Some more recent texts, from the 1920s and 1930s. Also get a "Dick and Jane" book. Someone should have them!

3. (optional) Provide sufficient copies of drawing paper so students can illustrate the values they wish to see transmitted.

Unit interaction: Senior high-Adult. Allow at least twenty minutes for examination of the books. If participants are having difficulty locating value messages, you might ask such questions as: What are the roles of males and females in the book? Are certain types of stories emphasized (such as war narratives, biographies of political leaders, etc.)? Are controversial topics treated in depth or avoided? Encourage specific answers. Participants will be tempted to say that the books encourage honesty or punctuality. Find out *how* each book defines honesty, or *why* it stresses being on time.

Evaluation: Through discussion, comments, and drawings, see if students grasp the notion that the school system reflects the demands of society. The comments made in discussion may indicate to what degree the participants feel alienated from the institution of schooling.

Suggestions: An interesting alternative activity is to gather a collection of student handouts and analyze them for value messages.

DEVELOPING *YOUR* VALUES EDUCATION STYLE

If you agree that everybody will teach values and that values will permeate every subject, either implicitly or explicitly, you should then ask yourself "How will I choose to approach values education?"

The following discussion will describe some alternatives for you to choose from. It begins with models traditionally practiced, details some philosophical ideals, and concludes with a description of the values investment teacher model, the investment manager.

Typical Teaching Styles

Two leaders of the values clarification movement, Merrill Harmin and Sidney Simon, have delineated three general styles you might adopt as a values educator.[14] First, you may choose to ignore values questions. Second, you could transmit certain values which you regard as vital. Third, you might decide to help students identify and better express their own values. Harmin and Simon dismiss the first style, arguing that it is impossible to ignore values.

While Harmin and Simon portray teachers you and I have known, and in the process reveal their preferences, Theodore Sizer speaks more in the abstract about four possible "perspectives" you may assume as a values educator.[15] You could choose to be a civic educator, upholding the standards of our culture. Or you may operate in the tradition of Socrates, constantly raising questions about the nature of truth. Or you might slowly nurture students through their "stages of moral development," providing models of good citizens for them to emulate.[16] Finally, you might function as a sociologist, helping students weigh the actions of various groups.

Let me blend some of their ideas and add a few of my own about the ways teachers often attempt to shape the values of students. As you read them, jot down your responses to such questions as: Am I using that style? Do I want to use that style? What does that style remind me of?

The Picture Perfect Teacher

The teacher serves as a personal model for what is proper behavior. This teacher selects curricular materials which extensively use biographical stories of famous people whom the teacher regards as "good" people.

The Gold-Star Teacher

Through the use of verbal and nonverbal clues such as gold-star rewards and threats of punishment, the teacher indicates what is expected of students. When value questions are discussed, solutions are frequently couched in "either-or" language.

The Wise Owl Teacher

The teacher uses a lot of "whos" and "whys." He asks why certain things have been done and wants the class members to explain, logically, what is right and what is wrong. While explanations and the use of rationality are necessary in all learning, the Wise Owl Teacher uses them to get students to accept what he has already decided is proper.

The Travel Agent

This teacher assumes that a wide reading of the "best" literature in the human odyssey will result in more humanely educated students. The teacher might suggest that the students engage in numerous activities to find out what they value, but often such experiences are in a "safe" range of alternatives.

The Detective

In this case the teacher functions like Joe Friday, the *Dragnet* detective, just after the facts. Simple answers are never enough. The teacher forces the student to probe any statement made about what is good or desirable behavior. In many ways this role is like that suggested by Postman and Weingarter, the "crap detector."[17] With this style the teacher rarely reveals his or her own point of view.

The Clarifier

Unlike the Detective, the teacher in this mold will frequently share or affirm his or her personal values. However, the teacher will also be careful not to force personal choices on students. The emphasis in this style is not on transmitting specific values as much as on training students in value-processing skills.[18]

You have probably had individual teachers who represent each of these styles. Most were a blend of several styles. Is it likely you will follow one style, or be a blend? If you think you will be a blend, what percentages of several styles would you like to have?

Another Approach: The Investment Manager

Throughout this book the point is made that there are a variety of ways to approach values education as well as a plethora of materials. What is essential is that you determine for yourself the style that fits you most comfortably. What you select might well be based on your educational environment.

I have found the approach described below to be successful *for me*. Because of that success, I have developed a number of strategies which relate to that approach. But I do not expect everyone to adopt this model.

What comparisons are there between an investment manager or broker and a teacher of values education? First, the educator should be a person who has been a long-time investor. You would hardly expect to do business with a broker who had no assets himself. And certainly you would have serious reservations about using the advice of an investment manager who could not reveal that he had obtained profitable returns from his initial investments. This doesn't mean that the teacher has to constantly "blow his horn." It simply means that the teacher should be able to communicate that he or she has invested substantially in life and that the returns have been most satisfying.

Second, the investment manager motif suggests a "service" relationship between the teacher and the student. The manager's livelihood depends upon the ability to satisfy the interests of the customer. The broker is an expert to whom the client turns. But the manager does not use this authority as a club. For the teacher, then, the task is to find out what the student is genuinely interested in pursuing, while avoiding the unsettling question "Why do you want to do that?" Martin Buber spoke to this point by calling the interaction between teacher and student a *dialogue.* Dialogue, for Buber, meant much more than two individuals talking *at* each other. Both participants need to make a maximum effort to understand the contributions and limitations of the other.[19]

Third, the investment manager's basic function is to continually review the performance of stocks and bonds in the marketplace. The manager cannot always rely upon past performance to predict how successful a certain mutual fund might be, for example. The advantages and pitfalls of various investment programs also have to be learned so the broker can explain the options to the customer. Likewise, the teacher should know the ways to approach value issues. The teacher can alert students to the "costs" of their choices, psychologically, physically, and financially. Further, the teacher's responsibility is to alert students to the diversity of stances others have taken, and the materials the student might use to reach a decision.

Fourth, the investment manager is a counselor who periodically meets with the individual client to discuss and evaluate the status of the customer's investments. The conscientious broker will give careful attention to the needs and future goals of the client. By training and by expectation, teachers in public and nonpublic schools are also evaluators. They are expected to learn the capabilities and restrictions of their students so they can plan for the individuals under their care. Fantini and Weinstein suggest that certain educators pay too much attention to meeting the *interests* of students and do not pay enough attention to the *needs* of students.[20]

The accountability movement in education demands that this point be expanded. The teacher is not a totally independent business person in charge of his own agency, like some investment managers. Teachers are expected to teach certain skills and produce certain payoffs. I believe teachers can use the accountability movement to clarify for themselves the dimensions in the affective domain they wish to explore and to evaluate with their students. You may decide that students need to know how to defend their value choices, or you may believe that students should be made more aware of the values of other cultural groups. Theologian Paul Tillich once commented that one task of religious educators was not to give right answers but to help students ask the right questions (which, for him, meant questions about what was ultimately good).[21]

Fifth, a typical characteristic of an investment broker is the willingness to risk. The qualities of self-confidence, trust in others, curiosity, and a desire for excitement are all components of the personality which asks others to make large commitments. Don't good teachers exhibit these same qualities? This doesn't necessarily mean that you have to be constantly trying new things, but you will find that students appreciate the attitude that a teacher has taken some risks with his own life and is willing to help students explore new territory.

To repeat, I find this model appropriate for me. It may not suit you or your educational environment. I do ask you to review the type of educator you are and then to choose value strategies which relate honestly to that approach. The following activity may help you find out how you think value issues should be approached in school.

Value Activity: "The Governor's Parade"

Assume you are a classroom teacher in Iron City. The big event of the day will be the governor's visit to the city. His motorcade is to pass within two blocks of the school.

There are mixed feelings about the governor in the community. He has recently signed into law an ecology bill which resulted in some local unemployment in certain factories.

There has been some talk in the teachers' lounge that angry citizens might be present at the parade to protest his decision. As you are about to begin your class, you receive a memo from the administration stating that it is up to each teacher to make a decision about having class discussions on the governor's decision and/or taking his or her class to the parade.

What would you do if some students asked to discuss the governor's decision? Or if they asked to go to the parade?

Value identification: "The Governor's Parade."

Activity: After voicing their decisions about the student requests, participants should discuss whether their statements reflect their general attitudes toward their approach to values education.

Learning aid: Story "The Governor's Parade."

Unit interaction: Participants are encouraged, if in a group, to share their decisions. If participants choose to pass, they should not be pressured to speak.

Evaluation: Leader might make a record of the variety of responses, from those which tend to fall back upon rules (the administration memo) to those which believe the teacher should encourage free expression of speech and action to those which stress being aware of the diverse views in the community and urging a "cool it" attitude.

Suggestions: The story can be altered to make it more violent. The parade turns into a shouting match when the governor's car stops. What if students want to go then?

ACTIVITIES FOR STUDENTS

The values activities presented so far have been designed for you, the reader. They reflect the values investment approach.

The two strategies which follow are general value activities which could be modified to fit many of the teaching styles described earlier. How would you structure either of these activities with a class? What does that tell you about your preferred style(s)?

Values Activity (Elementary): "The School Day"

Created by Jerry Hoffman

During your school day you meet a lot of people. Each of them will probably tell you something that is very important, at least to them. Sometimes they tell you through words, but other times they give you "messages" through the expression in their eyes or the way they dress.

What do you remember from each of the people you met today that was important, *to them or to you?*

Members of your family:

The busdriver:

Kids on the bus:

The school custodian:

The school secretary:

The principal:

Your teacher:

Other teachers:

School nurse:

Cooks at school:

Values Activity (Secondary): "Yearbook"

You have probably looked at several high school yearbooks by now. Let's pretend that this format is the one which will be used in your yearbook. How would you fill it out?

	You	Your best friend of the same sex	Your favorite teacher	A friend of the opposite sex
Pictures or sketches	◯	◯	◯	◯
1. Name or nickname:				
2. Significant facts:				
3. Outstanding single quality:				
4. School award:				
5. Future plans				

Questions to consider with the categories:

1.   Does the name used reveal how formal or informal you tend to be? Does the name used for each of the others reveal how well you know them?

2.   Do you really know the basic facts about the individuals you identified? Height? Weight? Income? How important are those facts?

3.   Are the qualities you selected widely known by others, or do you have "privileged" information? Do you associate with individuals who tend to have the same qualities?

4.   Would the individuals you named receive some of the typical school awards: most popular, most likely to succeed? What award would you give them?

5.   Was it difficult to identify the goals of everyone? If you are guessing, why not ask the individuals, to see how close you were to their plans? Do you find yourself choosing people who have similar vocational fields in mind and/or similar hobbies?

YOUR DECISION ABOUT VALUES EDUCATION

In this chapter you have read arguments for and against values education in the public schools. The point made by many other writers and by me is that it is virtually *impossible* to avoid values education. Historically, psychologically, the schools are in the values business.

If that is the case then you must face this question: How shall I approach values education? A number of teaching styles have been suggested. You may choose one of those or a combination of models.

My hope is that, whatever your choice, you have made your decision based on considerable thought.

Notes

1.   For a newspaper account describing the spread of values education, see the *New York Times*, April 30, 1975. A recent major effort of the National Education Association has been in-service programs for teachers. Historically, the organization is noted for its emphasis on moral and spiritual values being taught in the schools. See the Educational Policies Commission, *Moral and Spiritual Values in the Public Schools* (Washington, D.C.: National Education Association, 1951). For a more recent attempt to prepare teachers to cope with values questions, see Lawrence Metcalf, ed., *Values Education* (Washington, D.C.: National Council for Social Studies Yearbook, 1971). State educational agency responses are typified by the report, California State Board of Education, "Handbook on the Legal Rights and Responsibilities of School Personnel and Students in the Areas of Moral and Civic Education and Teaching about Religion," January 12, 1973. The state of Minnesota has an extensive set of guidelines for teacher candidates on the study of human relations they are to have in their preservice curriculum.

2.   R. Freeman Butts, "Assaults on a Great Idea," *The Nation* (April 30, 1973): 553–60.

3. American Association of School Administrators, *Religion in the Public Schools* (New York: Harper Chapelbooks, 1964).

4. "Moral Education," *Phi Delta Kappan* 55, no. 10 (June, 1975). Most articles in this issue are devoted to the topic of values education. Diane Divoky, "Affective Education: Are We Going Too Far?" *Learning* 4, no. 2 (October 1975): 20–27.

5. David Tyack, *Turning Points in American Educational History* (Waltham, Mass.: Blaisdell, 1967); Lawrence Cremin, *American Education: The Colonial Experience (1607–1783)* (New York: Harper, 1970); and Michael Katz, *Class, Bureaucracy and Schools: The Illusion of Educational Change in America* (New York: Praeger, 1971).

6. Clifton Johnson, *Old-Time Schools and School-books* (New York: Dover, 1963).

7. Horace Mann, "Twelfth Annual Report of the Board of Education together with the Twelfth Annual Report of the Secretary of the Board" (Boston: Dutton and Wentworth, 1849).

8. National Education Association Commission on the Reorganization of Secondary Education, *Cardinal Principles of Secondary Education* (Washington, D.C.: United States Bureau of Education, Bulletin No. 35, 1918).

9. United States Office of Education, The Commission on Life Adjustment Education for Youth, Federal Security Agency, *Life Adjustment Education for Every Youth* (Washington, D.C.: 1947).

10. Educational Policies Commission, *Moral and Spiritual Values*. Pages 8-11 portray life in that time as being "disordered" and acknowledge the paradox of "technological triumphs" and "social disasters."

11. The "classic" text is Louis Raths, Merrill Harmin, and Sidney Simon, *Values and Teaching* (Columbus, Ohio: Charles E. Merrill, 1966; 2nd ed., 1977).

12. A. S. Neill, *Summerhill* (New York: Hart, 1960). Summerhill is the English school which, according to Neill, has as its fundamental educational belief that training the emotion is more important than training the intellect.

13. John Holt, "The Values We Teach in School," *Teacher* (September, 1969); reprinted in Sidney B. Simon and Howard Kirschenbaum, eds., *Readings in Values Clarification* (Minneapolis: Winston, 1973), pp. 31–37.

14. Merrill Harmin and Sidney Simon, "Values." THE TEACHER'S HANDBOOK, Edited by Dwight W. Allen and Eli Seifman. Copyright © 1971 by Scott, Foresman and Company. Reprinted by permission. Reprinted in Simon and Kirschenbaum, eds., *Readings*, pp. 4–16.

15. Theodore R. Sizer, "Values Education in the Schools: A Practitioner's Perspective," *Religious Education* 70: no. 2 (March-April 1975), pp. 138–40. Reprinted from the March-April 1975 issue of *Religious Education* by permission of the publisher, The Religious Education Association, 409 Prospect St., New Haven, Ct., 06510. Membership or subscription available for $20.00 per year.

16. C. M. Beck, ed., *Moral Education* (Toronto: University of Toronto Press, 1971). This is an excellent series of papers, including one by Lawrence Kohlberg.

17. Neil Postman and Charles Weingarter, *Teaching as a Subversive Activity* (New York: Dell, 1969).

18. Harmin and Simon, "Values," pp. 14–16.

19. Martin Buber, *Between Man and Man* (New York: Macmillan, 1965).

20. Gerald Weinstein and Mario Fantini, eds., *Toward Humanistic Education: A Curriculum of Affect* (New York: Praeger, 1970), pp. 19–23.

21. Paul Tillich, *Theology of Culture* (New York: Galaxy Books, 1965 edition), pp. 201–13.

Learning and Teaching About Values

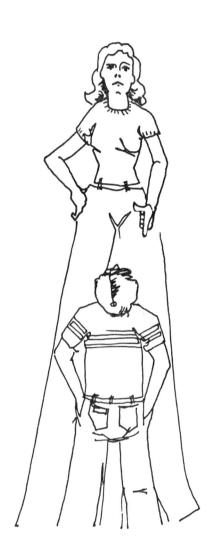

How did you learn your values? Who taught them to you? Can you recall times when you made dramatic changes in your value positions? Just what are values? How can you teach about values in a school?

Let's look at these important questions now, but I'll warn you in advance that I won't guarantee we can satisfactorily answer them all. We'll begin by surveying the ways in which "experts" define values, attitudes, and beliefs. Next we'll review the findings of researchers who have tried to uncover how individuals learn and change their values.

Most of the chapter, however, will reveal how these theories are related to nine approaches of values education. The review of each approach will begin with a statement on the goal of values education of that "school of thought," followed by a brief description of its proposed teacher model and commonly used teaching techniques, and a brief notation of the approach's advocates and/or researchers. Each description will conclude with a sample value activity. Coupled with the discussion in chapter 1 about teaching styles, you should be able to more clearly assess your own approach to values education.

WHAT ARE VALUES?

Cereal boxes advertise nutritional values, gasoline stations promote tire values, churches focus on eternal values, and the schools and the military are asked to shape values. What are they, and are they different from attitudes and beliefs?

Definitions

A survey of psychological and philosophical sources indicates that five general definitions of values are widely agreed upon.

For some, values are *eternal or universal truths,* believed to be passed down by some supernatural power.[1] To those who support this definition, values are divine imperatives to be transmitted by parents and teachers to the next generation. Debate about values and the role of the teacher, or authority figure, is kept to a minimum.

Values can also be defined as *needs.*[2] Our inner drives for such things as love, food, and shelter are fixed early in life, and many of our daily routines seek to provide these necessities. One publishing company, Steck-Vaughn of Austin, Texas, introduces its *Human Value Series* with this definition of values: "The basic wants and needs common to every human being—whoever he is and wherever he may be."[3]

Another popular definition of value is a *preference or benefit.* This definition would accept the concept that values can be objects or types of behaviors. Nicolas Rescher, after an extensive survey of value theories and definitions, reduced his personal definition to one compatible with this outlook. Values, he claimed, are "disposition clusters."[4]

Many sociologists and anthropologists define values as the *standards or rules* of a society. This definition is broad enough to encompass both the abstract (justice, honesty) and the specific (laws and virtues, such as punctuality). Advocates of this definition would see human beings as rule-following animals who basically wish to live in harmony with their fellow human beings.[5] This definition would be widely accepted by those who believe society needs to recapture lost values, or those who believe we need to build better communications.

Raths, Harmin, and Simon claim that it is more important to be concerned about the *valuing process* than the definition of a value.[6] They have developed seven criteria in the valuing process which they claim must be met before you can have a value.

1. Values must be freely determined.
2. Thoughtful consideration must be given to the choice of a value.
3. Real alternatives must exist from which to choose.
4. Values will elicit a positive feeling.
5. Values will be publically affirmed.

6. A person will expend resources, such as time, money, reputation, on his values.

7. Lifestyles will reveal a person's values.

One advocate of the values clarification approach, Howard Kirschenbaum, has raised some questions about the validity of these seven criteria.[7] His primary arguments center on points **1, 5,** and **6.** When is a person ever sure that he or she has freely chosen something? Can't one quietly share his values with friends without publicity? What of the donor who wishes to remain anonymous so that the spotlight remains on the cause he supports? Kirschenbaum then says that the matter of degree of support is far too nebulous. In addition to raising questions about the seven criteria, Kirschenbaum also comments on the imbalance of cognitive and affective components in the values clarification approach.

You may be frustrated now, realizing that there is no widespread agreement on what constitutes a value. But don't despair so much that you blindly give in to some curriculum manual and follow it slavishly.

Beliefs, Attitudes, and Values

Because some educators feel they are presenting materials which touch upon the likes, the preferences, and the choices people make, and because they are using a values book, they believe they are "doing" values education. That is not necessarily true. Actually, they may be doing "attitude" education or "belief" instruction.

Consider the following explanations of the differences between attitudes, beliefs, and values.

Fishbein and Raven argue that there are two types of belief, both being forms of probability.[8] Using the example of extrasensory perception (ESP), they indicate that you can believe *in* it, based on your assessment of the report of witnesses. You can also believe something *about* it, that it is supernatural. Attitudes are built from facts. You could then advocate that people ought to engage in ESP. Finally, a value would be your commitment to it, through actual exercise of ESP.

Rokeach, in *Beliefs, Attitudes, and Values,* offers a different framework for distinguishing between the three terms. Rokeach says beliefs "are inferences made by an observor about underlying states of expectancy."[9] For him, there are three types of belief: descriptive ("I believe the sun rises in the east"); evaluative ("I believe that ice cream is good"); and prescriptive ("I believe children ought to obey their parents"). While Fishbein and Raven, and other researchers such as Krech and

Crutchfield, claim beliefs are neutral in affect, Rokeach argues that all beliefs are predispositions to actions.[10]

An attitude, according to Rokeach, "is a relatively enduring organization of beliefs around an object or situation predisposing one to respond in some preferential manner."[11] In other words, attitudes are clusters of beliefs. But not all beliefs are necessarily attitudes.

Rokeach concludes that a value, unlike an attitude, is a single belief that guides actions and judgments.

> A value . . . is an imperative to action, not only a belief about the preferable, but also a preference for the preferable. Finally, a value, unlike an attitude, is a standard or yardstick to guide actions . . . and [a] justification of [the actions of] self and others.[12]

The crucial element in both attempts to define terms is that the value category involves *action,* or at least the revelation of a refusal to act.

Value: Generated Action, Deliberate Nonactivity

I am inclined to accept a categorization of beliefs, attitudes, and values similar to Rokeach's. Beliefs are primarily collections of facts and opinions about what is thought to be true. Attitudes are clustered beliefs which proclaim what is of significance (what is good, beautiful, or needed). *Values are those combinations of attitudes which generate action or deliberate choice to avoid action.*

As the illustration reveals, our individual beliefs, or perceptions of what we hold is true, merge like roads into a traffic circle, forming attitudes. As events confront us we must stop and make decisions. The resulting actions, or choices to not participate, are our values. Obviously, as we have many attitudes, so we have many values.

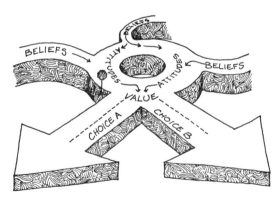

Figure 2–1   *Beliefs, Attitudes, Values*

This definition embodies several philosophical and pedagogical viewpoints.

First, it accepts the concept that beliefs, attitudes, and values are interdependent, but can be separated.

Second, it adopts the position that valuing cannot be isolated from acting or decision making at some point. What should be underscored here is that it does not have to be an overt action. The other side of the "action coin" is that you may at times deliberately decide not to change what you are doing, or you deliberately resist charting a new activity which has been suggested to you.

The implication of this definition of a value (and values education) is that the educator must be prepared to go beyond talking about values or only being concerned about presenting facts for students to make decisions. Sooner or later, some of the value decisions students have made, and their consequences, will surface. To me, the dedicated teacher will systematically plan how discussion on student actions will be carried on in the classroom. Moreover, plans for action projects and periodic evaluations will have to be included.[13]

You should determine what distinctions you make between the three terms, for it will make a difference in your approach to teaching about values. If you are concerned that students do not have enough information to make wise decisions, and if you further believe that the school should not impose one certain set of personal values upon students, you may stress "belief instruction." On the other hand, you may feel that your primary task, as an educator, is to mold the attitudes of your charges toward a subject matter or a type of activity (Students should appreciate Shakespeare. Merit badge requirements are meaningful). In both cases you may be quite content to begin the valuing process, and just assume that actual changes are occurring in the students' behavior.

To be truly involved in values education is to be truly concerned about the actions students take. As an educator who believes values will be exhibited, you should consciously or unconsciously plan your approach to values education so that students have many opportunities to reveal what they have decided to do, or what they have decided *not* to do.

Value Activity: "First Impressions"

To gain some insight into what you believe and what you will act upon, try the following activity with the help of a friend. Have your friend locate a newspaper or magazine picture which depicts some conflict situation. Pictures on sports, wars, business, and schooling would be appropriate.

When you look at the picture, what are your first impressions? How do you feel? What do you believe is happening? What would you do if you were at that scene? Now ask the friend to explain the story behind the picture.

Value identification: "First Impressions."

Activity: After orally interpreting a photographic situation and hearing the actual story behind it, the participant delineates between his or her beliefs, attitudes, and values regarding the situation depicted.

Learning aids: A photograph.

Unit interaction: See description above.

Evaluation: In addition to discussing the questions above, you might note the discrepancy between your version of what went on and what actually occurred. Focus on what you actually would *do*.

Suggestions: There are several formal sets of pictures which would help you and your students gain insights into your prejudices. An especially good set is found in "Images of People," *Sociological Resources for the Social Studies* (Boston: Allyn & Bacon, 1969), pp. 9–14. Augsburg Press has a set, "Created Male and Female," which allows you to explore your attitudes toward love and sex.

Make your own set of pictures of individuals and conflict situations. Try to gather pictures of important figures who are not well known.

HOW ARE VALUES LEARNED?

Perhaps more important than what values are is how we modify them and transmit them to others. It is important for you to become aware of the general theories regarding value and attitude change if you are an educator. I find it necessary to include the research both on value and on attitude change because they are so closely related.

Any attempt to categorize values theories is arbitrary. The following format shows a perspective different from mine which is nevertheless provocative. It has been developed by the staff of Research for Better Schools, Inc. This format was the basis for discussions about the future of moral education at a conference in Philadelphia in June, 1976, sponsored by RBS and the National Institute of Education.

Four theoretical approaches were identified. The cognitive-decision theorists are primarily philosophers, such as R. S. Peters and John Wilson, who believe that a variety of processes are involved in value decision making. Self-interest, consideration for others, a regard for reason, and cultural wisdom are just a few. They favor philosophical techniques for ethical decision making.

The developmental theorists, like Lawrence Kohlberg, are usually psychologists. They are more prone to hold that age-related stages of moral development need to be considered. Their emphasis is upon moral judgment rather than action.

Research psychologists, such as Ervin Staub, form another camp called the *prosocial* theorists, according to the Research for Better Schools schema. Individuals are viewed as objects to be manipulated and trained in socially acceptable ways. Through role taking and intense discussions on such values as altruism, cooperation, and empathy, the participants learn how to generate more helpful behaviors.

The largest group are the values theorists. The distinctive beliefs of this group of educators, psychologists, and sociologists are that values are central to life and that consciously raising value issues will in fact promote changes in behavior.

Theories of Valuing

Modeling

The most frequently mentioned theory of how people learn their values is modeling. According to this view, we learn our values through exposure to people around us. Such research institutions as the Harvard Center for Infant Education claim that it is the association with an adult during the crucial age of fifteen to eighteen months that will determine how creative an individual will be.[14] Psychologists such as Erik Erikson, writing in *Childhood and Society,* suggest that our closest associates— parents, relatives, and later, peers—serve as templates. Through observation and mimicry over the years, we learn such characteristics as basic trust or mistrust of other individuals, as well as autonomy or dependency and responsibility or irresponsibility.[15]

The key to this theory of valuing is that values are transmitted not so much by word of mouth as by day-to-day living. This includes giving commands, however. Children are expected to follow orders, and there is little effort made to explain *why* this is the way things ought to be done. The fact that the adult does it this way is to be accepted as justification for the behavior.

Training

A similar theory of valuing is training or persuasion. This theory assumes that individuals want to become a part of society and, in fact, want to be active contributors. They want to understand the community rules and rituals.[16]

What separates this approach from the modeling theory is that training is much more attuned to active teaching than incidental instruction. Educators using this technique would deliberately spell out the rules of the game, requiring students to defend their choices and build rational courses of action. Where modeling asserts this is the way you act (and don't ask questions why), training encourages participants to think through possible avenues of behavior.

A leading proponent of this second approach is Lawrence Kohlberg, who is noted for his six stages of moral development.[17] In his longitudinal studies done around the world, Kohlberg claims that individuals can improve their moral decision making if given sufficient training. His findings indicate that individuals progress from one stage to a higher stage; that the individuals can comprehend moral statements at the stage just above or below their stage, but that moral comments two stages below become "babyish" and two stages above are incomprehensible; and that learners are usually at one stage, although most have some "stage mix."

His six stages of moral development are:

Stage 1: punishment and obedience   Common for ages four through six, the person in this stage assumes that something is good if he or she is rewarded for doing it and bad if there is a punishment attached to it.

Stage 2: mutual benefit   This is sometimes called the "scratch my back, I'll scratch yours" stage. For the typical five- to seven-year-old, the best answer to a moral dilemma would be the one which permitted him or her to gain a favor in return for granting one.

Stage 3: role stereotype   This stage is popularly called the *sugar-spice* stage. Preteens to adults often use the reasoning of this level. Moral choices are based on what is expected. I will act a certain way because a male is supposed to act that way. Or if you are in a supervisor's role, you might say that your judgment was made because that is the fair way for a supervisor to treat a worker.

Stage 4: law and order   Most adults are in this category, according to Kohlberg. The typical response to a dilemma is "Do what the law says is right." People at stage 4 believe that anarchy will result if laws are not strictly enforced.

Stage 5: social contract Relatively few individuals attain this stage. Those who do temper their respect for the law with compassion and the belief that exceptions must be allowed. Kohlberg indicates that the United States Constitution is a prime example of stage 5 reasoning.

Stage 6: justice Only a few individuals will hold this stage consistently, according to Kohlberg. Living with your conscience is ultimately important, but it means that you would not act differently than you would wish others to act. If you engage in civil disobedience, you would be willing to accept punishment.[18]

Perhaps another way to describe the training approach is to say that many of its advocates would use such terms as "consciousness-raising" or "making people aware."

Behavior Modification

Some experts claim that a most effective way to change behavior is to use behavior modification techniques. Simply put, these techniques call for the changer to positively reinforce, or reward, the subject whenever the subject performs a positive action. For example, the parent will give the child money for music practice; the teacher will praise the reluctant reader for books completed; and students will show more attention when the dull lecturer is enthusiastic.

Proponents of behavior modification deny the charge that it is a form of bribery, because bribery involves coercing someone to do something illegal.[19] Another charge leveled at behavioral modification is that it is deceitful manipulation. The behaviorist would answer that *all* educators seek to influence the behavior of their students. Values educators must face this question. To what degree is it compatible with your approach to values education to consciously or unconsciously manipulate the activities of your students?[20]

Cognitive Dissonance

A growing trend, especially in the realm of attitude change, is known as the *cognitive dissonance* technique. According to the early research of Festinger, expanded by Milton Rokeach, dramatic changes in values and attitudes will occur when individuals are confronted by the inconsistencies between what they say they value, and what they actually value. Some will deny their former positions; others will amend their current actions.[21]

A famous experiment by Rokeach involved giving students a rank-order questionnaire on eighteen values. Many ranked freedom first and equality in the middle range. In a follow-up discussion it was pointed out that these choices showed they valued freedom for themselves, but not for others. Some of the participants were later sent letters of invitation from a civil rights group and, compared with a control group, a significantly greater number did join or sent a contribution.

Several points from this research should be stressed. A significant finding is that individuals who make public pronouncements on an issue will be less inclined to change that position than those who have not made some public statement, even when they are presented with data which indicate the position was based on inaccurate information. This can be construed as a warning to all value educators to urge students not to make premature public affirmations. Rokeach has indicated, moreover, that this technique is fairly new. In the past most research instruments have been concerned with individuals' feelings about objects (for example, free enterprise, ecology), rather than about how people would react in specific situations.

Goal-Setting

Goal-setting is still another method which has proved effective in changing individuals' actions. As revealed in the work of William Glasser, a psychiatrist from Los Angeles, most individuals want to lead productive lives.[22] The delinquent girls he counselled had poor self-images and downgraded their chances for success.

Glasser, like Abraham Maslow, believes that individuals should be guided toward "self-actualized" lives.[23] Through work in small groups, participants discuss their life goals and help each other set realistic goals with deadlines. Consequences for not completing the goals are also incorporated in the discussions. According to Glasser, this approach resulted in marked improvement in the girls. Rather than excusing themselves or their families or blaming society for problems, they took on responsibilities and made gains in abilities as well as self-concepts.

Behavior Patterns

Some researchers conclude that attitude changes in individuals can be produced by merely pointing to their *behavior patterns*.[24] While they may have begun these patterns quite innocently or accidentally, the subjects may come to report them as their conscious preferences if they are quizzed about them frequently enough. For example, suppose you were at a series of parties at which a new food was available. If someone questioned you about your eating it, you might begin to talk as though you had deliberately chosen it.

Ask yourself again how you have developed your values. Are you more aware of a gradual process of steady growth, or do you recall vivid key events which "turned you around"? What about those who most influenced you? Did they engage in modeling, training, or cognitive dissonance with you?

You should be asking yourself now, "What about my approach in the classroom? What will I do when I see students whose behavior I want to change? Will I do nothing? Which approach am I likely to adopt?"

HOW I FEEL ABOUT VALUES EDUCATION NOW

Now that we have surveyed some definitions of values and considered some theories, it is appropriate that we turn to a closer examination of the various approaches which embody these definitions and theories. The basic typology which I have modified and the identification of a number of resources in this section come from Douglas Superka of the Social Science Education Consortium.[25]

Before launching into the nine approaches I have identified, you might benefit from a pretest. Each of the nine statements below reflects a different goal for values education. On the continuum, you will note five numbers, each representing an attitude from "strongly agree" to "strongly disagree." For each statement representing one of the nine approaches, choose the number which most closely represents your feeling now.

1	2	3	4	5
Strongly agree	Somewhat agree	Neutral	Somewhat disagree	Strongly disagree

In my educational situation students should be taught to:

_____ **1.** Use logical thinking and scientific methods of collecting and analyzing data as the fundamental approach to determining value choices.

_____ **2.** Grasp the degrees of difference typically used by individuals in their value decisions and then develop their own internal ordering of moral reasoning.

_____ **3.** Respect and adopt the universal values on which this country was founded, so they might become contributing members of the nation.

_____   **4.** Develop positive self-concepts and pleasant relationships with peers and family.

_____   **5.** Weigh value options and consequences, become more aware of their own values, and more clearly state their personal value positions.

_____   **6.** Investigate and ACT upon ethical situations in their communities.

_____   **7.** Express more openly their spontaneous reactions to aesthetic stimuli and heighten their sensitivities to tastes, sounds, smells, and textures.

_____   **8.** Reflect upon the unity of the world (cosmos) and build their senses of inner contentment.

_____   **9.** Systematically explore a combination of cognitive and affective activities which move the students toward value decisions and actions.

Evaluate your answers now. Did you mark any one goal with a "1"? If so, you will probably feel comfortable with that approach for now. You may wish to look ahead and read about that approach. If you marked several goals with either "1" or "2" you are probably willing to try several approaches. Find out more about them and see if they mesh with your philosophy.

The goals and approaches are:

1. Value analysis.
2. Moral reasoning.
3. Transmission.
4. Integration.
5. Values clarification.
6. Action.
7. Evocation.
8. Union.
9. Values investment.

APPROACHES TO TEACHING ABOUT VALUES

Each of the nine approaches just listed will be described in the following format: goal, belief about human nature, teacher role, theorists, and sample activity.

See the end of this chapter for a matrix which summarizes various aspects of these approaches. The next chapter will list specific curriculum sets that follow the nine approaches.

1. Analysis

Goal   To train students to use logical thinking and scientific methods of collecting and analyzing data as the fundamental approach to determining their personal and society's values.

Human nature   The individual is regarded as a rational actor. Supporters would claim that society must stand upon rational foundations or else civility will be lost. Some support for this position comes from several cognitively oriented psychotherapists, Ellis and Kelly, who contend that good health requires a person to test his personal constructs both empirically and experimentally.[26]

Teacher role/teaching methods   The teacher is a guide to resources, a presenter of facts and positions, the challenger who asks students to defend their positions.

Analysis encourages frequent use of individual or group study of value issues through research projects and debates. The use of the inquiry method would be popular.[27]

Theorists   Michael Scriven of the University of California, Berkeley, is best known. In the public-school context, he claims that the rational approach is the only justifiable one. Pepper and Handy have also written in this field.[28]

Activity   From Jerrold R. Coombs and Milton Meux, *Values Education* (Washington, D.C.: National Council for the Social Studies, 1972).

Students are encouraged to make value decisions based on data analysis. For example, students do research on the topic of welfare and placed their findings on "evidence cards." As the illustrations indicate, students ascertain fact and opinion to build their positions. The thoughtful teacher would help students analyze their proposed solutions and correct their faulty data and stereotypes.

> Value judgment: Relief is morally wrong.
> Fact: Relief gives money to people who haven't earned it.
> Criterion: Practices that give money to people who haven't earned it are morally wrong.

Figure 2–2   *Simple evidence card*

	Point of View
Value Judgment: Relief is morally wrong.	Moral
Fact: Relief gives money to people who haven't earned it.	Moral
Criterion: Practices that give money to people who haven't earned it are morally wrong.	

Figure 2–3   *Simple evidence card with point of view*

Backing (Positive)	Contrary (Negative)
People on relief in Detroit receive $175 per month and have no jobs. People on relief in Chicago get $200 a month and do not have jobs.	Some people on relief work hard even though they don't have a job.

Figure 2–4   *Back of evidence card, with backing and contrary evidence for fact*

Backing (Positive)	Contrary (Negative)
People on relief in Detroit receive $175 a month and have no jobs. People on relief in Chicago get $200 a month and do not have jobs.	Some people on relief work hard even though they do not have jobs.
Reasons for believing criterion Such practices lower a person's dignity and self-esteem. Such practices keep a person from trying to improve himself or herself.	**Reasons for not believing criterion** It can't be morally wrong to raise people's standards of living when they are victims of a system over which they have no control.

Figure 2–5   *Back of evidence card, with backing and contrary evidence for the facts and reasons for and against the criterion*

2. Moral Reasoning

Goal   Through discussions, students are to realize the hierarchy of reasons on which moral choices can be made, and they are to develop their rational powers accordingly.

Human nature   Each person can be an active initiator of moral decisions. Rather than blindly accepting what is right and wrong, individuals can learn and internalize various responses to moral situations.

Teacher role/learning methods   If you were a teacher applying this approach, you would be an *arranger,* giving much attention to the selection of stories which could elicit a variety of responses rather than a single right answer. Also, you would be a questioner, calling for each student to think through his choices and to determine if each was his own decision or due to pressure from others around him.

The most popular teaching device is the moral dilemma situation. Dilemmas can be portrayed in a variety of media—filmstrips, pictures, or written accounts. Usually the class breaks up into small groups for discussions, which tend to be relatively structured and argumentative.

Theorists   Kohlberg's stages of moral development are the framework of many programs today. His work has been built upon the findings of Piaget, and is similar to the developmental views of Peck and Havighurst, Beck, and Loevinger.[29]

Activity   from Edmund V. Sullivan, *Moral Learning* (New York: Paulist Press, 1975), p. 3 (a dilemma from Lawrence Kohlberg).

The Druggist
and the Husband

In Europe a woman was near death from a special kind of cancer. There was one drug that the doctors thought might save her; it was a form of radium that a druggist in the same town had recently discovered. The drug was expensive to make, but the druggist was charging ten times what the drug cost him to make. He paid $200 for the radium and charged $2,000 for a small dose of the drug. The sick woman's husband, Heinz, went to everyone he knew to borrow the money, but he could only get together about $1,000 which is half of what it cost. He told the druggist that his wife was dying and asked him to sell it cheaper or let him pay later. But the druggist said, "No, I discovered the drug and I'm going to make money from it." So Heinz got desperate and broke into the man's store to steal the drug for his wife. Should Heinz have done that? Was it actually wrong or right? Why?

Student responses to this story include: "He shouldn't take the drug because he will get caught" (stage 1) and "He has an obligation to his wife" (stage 5).

3. Transmission

Goal   To instill in students both a respect for and a desire to adopt the universal values on which this country was founded, so that they might become contributing members of society.

Human nature   The individual is seen as a reactor rather than an initiator, at times likened to clay that is to be formed into a desirable shape and at other times thought of as a mischievous receptacle to be filled with insight. Typically, societal needs are regarded as more important than individual needs.

Teacher role/learning styles   In this case, you as a teacher would serve as a model of what is best in society. Using reprimands and rewards, you would guide students toward commonly accepted virtues of the nation.

The instructional methods often used are lecture, panels, films, and open-ended stories which suggest certain answers. Frequently, the stories chosen narrate the heroic deeds of past leaders or contemporary men and women who are "successful."

Theorists   Many curricular programs in this approach are based on lists of so-called *universal* values and contain many traditional terms. For example, the Steck-Vaughn Company *Human Values* series is organized around the eight values identified by psychologist Harold Laswell: affection, respect, power, wealth, enlightenment, skill, well being, and rectitude.[30] Others whose findings are used to support this approach include sociologist Talcott Parsons and psychologists Maslow and Sears.[31]

Activity   Lesson on religious prejudice, from Joan M. Sayre, *Teaching Moral Values Through Behavior Modification*—Intermediate Level (Danville, Illinois: The Interstate Printers & Publishers, Inc., 1972), p. 8.

All of the students in Miss Foster's class at Riverside School were invited to a Thanksgiving play at St. Mary's. Since St. Mary's was so far away, Miss Foster arranged for the school bus to take them after lunch. Marilyn and her friend Janet, wanted to sit together on the bus. They ate their lunch quickly and went to stand in line at the front door, as Miss Foster had told them to do.

Finally it was time to leave, and all of the students boarded the bus. They sang school songs as they drove along the highway.

When they arrived at St. Mary's, they were surprised to see a lady in a strange-looking black-and-white dress come out to greet them. Marilyn and Janet looked at each other and started to giggle, but they stopped when they saw Miss Foster turn around and look at them with disapproval.

As they went into the school auditorium, they noticed a statue of a man wearing a long black robe. They had never seen anything like this. Marilyn said, "Isn't that dumb, having a statue inside the school instead of out in front?" Janet nodded her head in agreement and mentioned that she thought the man's clothes looked silly, too.

After they had taken their seats, the students from St. Mary's marched into the auditorium. Janet stared at them in amazement. All of the students were dressed exactly alike. The girls wore blue skirts, white blouses, and light blue socks. The boys were dressed in white shirts and blue slacks. Janet poked Marilyn and said, "They look like a bunch of prisoners to me," and both of the girls laughed. They thought it was so funny that both girls turned to the persons sitting next to them and repeated the remark in a whisper. Soon the whole row was giggling. Miss Foster looked shocked and walked down the aisle to the row where the girls were sitting. They stopped laughing immediately, sat up, and looked straight ahead. "I want to see you two girls when we get back to school," Miss Foster told them.

What do you think Miss Foster said to the girls?

Is it polite to laugh at anyone's beliefs and customs?

What are some things in your school, home, and community that might look strange to an outsider?

The illustrations by June A. Howard which accompany the story make it clear that the expected response of the girls is to be that of regret. The obvious answer to the question "Is it polite to laugh at anyone's beliefs and customs?" is a decided no.

4. Integration

Goal Students are to develop positive self-concepts and build pleasant relationships with peers and family. The primary emphasis is often on building self-enhancement through discussions about personal feelings.

Human nature The individual is believed to be the source of what is good and acceptable. Given opportunities for growth, the individual will choose what is personally satisfying and healthy for society. There are similarities between integration and transmission. The difference is that while the transmission approach puts the society first, integration stresses self-acceptance first and adjustment to society second.

Teacher role/learning styles   Your first task as a teacher is to communicate to the students that they are worthwhile, that they each have both assets and limitations and should feel free to express their viewpoints and attitudes. Hence, you are an *accepter.*

Teacher manuals usually suggest such learning aids and techniques as posters, puppet plays, and group discussions, which encourage the sharing of feelings and the solving of group and individual problems.

Theorists   A number of writers in the field of counseling would be representative of this approach. Included are Carl Rogers, Haim Ginott, and Thomas Harris.[32]

Activity   Puppet story from DUSO Kit #1 (Developing Understanding of Self and Others), Don Dinkmeyer, "Duso Talks about Friends" (Circle Pines, Minnesota: American Guidance Service, 1970). Reprinted by permission of American Guidance Service, Inc.

The Duso the Dolphin stories often highlight the uniqueness of each individual. This particular story describes what happens, however, when someone wants to be too much of an individual. The children hear the voice of Duso on a tape and the teacher has a flip chart with several pictures matching the story.

Hellooooooooooo, boys and girls! It's your old friend from the sea, Duso the Dolphin. Your teacher tells me that you are going to be talking about sharing . . . and helping others . . . and about friends.

If you will listen carefully, I will tell you about some of *my* friends down at the bottom of the sea.

One thing that we have learned is everybody needs to *have friends.* We just can't get along without friends. You may have heard of a fish named Sharky. Well, one time Sharky tried to get along without friends.

Sharky is not a very friendly fish anyway. He has terrible manners and he gets mad about almost anything. Some of the fish decided that they would rather not be friends with Sharky. Sharky said that he didn't care and he didn't need any friends at all.

It wasn't long, though, until Sharky was so lonesome that he didn't care about eating or playing or swimming—anything. He just moped around the bottom of the sea with a sad look on his long face. I think old Sharky would have just died if it hadn't been for the little pilot fish.

When those little striped fish saw how lonely Sharky was, they felt sorry for him. They began to play with Sharky and go places with him. They were going to be friendly with Sharky even if he wasn't friendly with them! The pilot fish's friendship made Sharky feel much better. Now, he knows that everybody needs to have friends. He is not as grouchy and bad mannered as he used to be. We all like Sharky much better since he learned that everybody needs to have friends.

Another thing we have learned down at the bottom of the sea is that *friends help each other.*

Small children, from my experience, really like the puppet, Duso, and want to manipulate him. Usually I have found that the messages Duso brings about personal self-worth and group adjustment are repeated enthusiastically by the students.

5. Clarification

Goal   To introduce students to the skills of valuing and to teach them how to constantly reexamine their own values and reach their own decisions. More specifically, this approach uses a preponderance of cognitive self-analysis strategies, coupled with some emotional awareness activities, to teach students to weigh value options and express their own values.

Human nature   The person is seen as an initiator of his or her interaction with society and the environment. Similar to the integration point of view, clarification holds that no one knows better than the individual what is best for him. Internal rather than external forces should be the prime determinants of human behavior.

Teacher role/learning style   If you wish to be a "clarifier," you would have to develop two roles equally: one as a *trainer,* the other as a *sharer.* As a trainer you help students learn the techniques of questioning their own values and evaluating their stands. Yet you cannot stay apart from the "action," for a clarifier must also be willing to share and affirm your values.

Frequently value clarification strategies are put out in kits which emphasize rank-order activities, continuums, and values voting, and in diaries which ask readers to respond privately to brief questions.

Theorists   Louis Raths, the originator of the term *values clarification,* traces his philosophy back to John Dewey. Others who use this approach today include Sidney Simon and Shaftel and Shaftel.[33]

Activity   Value Sheet No, 6, "Friendship," Raths, Harmin, and Simon, *Values and Teaching,* 1966, p. 95.

1. What does friendship mean to you?
2. If you have friends, did you choose them or did they get to be your friends by accident?
3. In what ways do you show friendship?
4. How important do you think it is to develop and maintain friendships?
5. If you plan to make any changes in your ways, please say what changes you will make. If you do not intend to make any changes in your ways, write "No changes."

> Students are usually quite eager to carry on discussions relating to topics like this.

6. Action

Goal   While combining elements from several other values approaches, action's distinctive ingredient is its emphasis upon "results." It is not enough to think about values; the student is expected to seek out problems and actively work for their solutions.

Human nature   Students are not merely passive reactors but interactive members of a social group and system. To be fully human is to be fully involved with others in experiencing the joys and sorrows of life.

Teacher role/learning styles   Should you be drawn to this approach, your primary role would be that of *arranger.* You would help class members locate situations to investigate or perhaps arrange for trips and for speakers to represent varied points of view.

The activities used most often would be field trips, reports, and group projects—such as conferences with community leaders, publication of findings, and demonstrations.

Theorists   Much support for the action approach can be found in the writings of John Dewey. More recently, the work of Blumer in sociology and Sullivan and Bigge in psychology would relate to this approach.[34]

Activity   From W. Ron Jones, *Finding Community: A Guide to Community Research and Action* (Palo Alto, California: James E. Freel, 1971), pp. 26–29.

> Students are to study the similarities and differences in merchandise and credit costs between low-income and middle-income neighborhoods through field research. After comparing and contrasting such differences on specific items, such as radios and vacuum cleaners, the students discuss their results. Then they clarify how deeply they feel about their conclusions. The students are urged to consider and choose from among various alternatives of community action which would affirm the values reflected in their findings.
>
> If, for example, fraudulent and unfair practices have been uncovered and the student feels very strongly that these practices are wrong, he or she would choose one of the following action projects: (1) write and distribute a community "Buyer's Guide" describing product values and the cost of credit; (2) inform the neighborhood legal assistance office and inquire about the procedure for filing a

class suit against the store or finance agent; (3) write a letter of complaint to local news media and government officials; or (4) use guerilla theater to dramatize fraudulent commercial practices.[35]

According to reports I have heard, students are made more aware of the importance of personal investigations and do increasingly take part in more active ways.

7. Evocation

Goal   To have students express more openly and freely their spontaneous reactions to aesthetic stimuli and heighten their sensitivities to tastes, sounds, smells, and textures.

Human nature   An assumption consistently made by educators who favor this approach is that human beings want to be creative and expressive, but have been taught to stifle their feelings and creativity. For them, the most significant decisions in life are "based on emotion and intuition, not logic and rationality."[36]

Teacher role/learning styles   If you were committed to this approach, you would conceive of your first responsibility as being a *stimulator,* providing resources which were heavily laden with value messages or which required students to react sensually.

Posters and photographs, objects, and readings would be typical vehicles used to evoke discussion. Because some educators favoring this approach think there is far too much cognitive education now, highly structured lesson plans would be ruled out.

Theorists   Psychologists such as Combs and Snygg and Whitaker and Malone provide some underpinnings for this approach. Among educators, agreement would be found in Richard Jones, *Fantasy and Feeling in Education,* and Weinstein and Fantini, *Toward Humanistic Education.*[37]

Activity   "Hands to Hands," from Gloria A. Castillo, *Left-Handed Teaching* (New York: Praeger, 1974), p. 74.

Castillo has recommended the following approach for elementary students. Have the class pair up. Have the students lie down on their backs with heads touching. Each person is to then raise his hands so they will contact the hands of his partner.

Instructions to class: Have your hands say hello to your partner. Tell your partner how you feel now. Try to learn something about your partner through the shape and texture of his hands. Are they long and tapered? Are they smooth or rough? Can you convey an important message to your partner through your hands? Say goodbye to your partner.

If room conditions or other factors do not permit stretching out on the floor, you can do this seated back to back, with hands at the sides. It can be done with hands extended over the shoulders, but it becomes tiring.

When I have used this activity, usually with adults, the first reaction is one of embarrassment. For some college students there is then silliness or shyness. However, by the end of the activity, there is usually much involvement.

8. Union

Goal   To help students reflect upon the unity of the world (cosmos) and to build their senses of inner contentment or senses of "at-one-ness" with the universe.

Human nature   A wide range of philosophical and theological positions can fit under the Union umbrella, from those that hold the individual is a lost and sinful being who will only find fulfillment when he submits to a divine will, to those which stress that the individual only needs to find peace through meditation to place him on the universe's "wave-length." Mutually what these approaches stress is the interdependence of person and environment, thoughts and feelings, body and soul.

Teacher role/learning styles   If you are attracted to this approach, you would likely feel that the teacher is often a *harmonizer*, both a model for appropriate behavior and a resource for the eternal ideas. In large measure, the teacher's responsibility would be that of a technician who passes on the skills for the novice to use to reach union with the ultimate.

The techniques employed could include transcendental meditation, prayer, Zen Buddhism, self-hypnosis, dream analysis, mind-expanding drugs, and active, symbolic imagination.

Theorists   Paul Tillich would serve as a representative of liberal theology, while Watts would reflect some of the Eastern philosophy and Driscoll would be representative of TM.[38]

Activity   George Brown, *Human Teaching for Human Learning* (New York: The Viking Press, 1971), pp. 49–50).

[George] begins by asking the participants to relax, close their eyes, and "in fantasy go away someplace, someplace where you really would like to be, alone or with someone you like." (Two-minute pause.) "Now come back to the group, open your eyes, look around, and be aware not only of what you see but of how you see—how clear or bright colors are, for example." (One-minute pause.) "Close your eyes and go away again. You might go to the same place or perhaps someplace new. Do as you wish." (One-minute pause.) "Come back again and look around. Again be aware of how you are perceiving." (One-minute pause.) "Now in your own rhythm withdraw or stay here. You may want to withdraw for the rest of the time in this exercise, or you may want to stay here. Just allow yourself to tune in to what *you* really want, from moment to moment."

This process can be revealing for a number of participants. For others it is not cognitive enough.

9. Values Investment

Goal   To systematically aid students to explore value issues through a combination of cognitive and affective activities which require periodic action decisions.

Human nature   This perspective begins with the assumption that all people wish to have some meaning or significance in their lives. How they act depends on how they perceive the meaning of the world and themselves. While this approach celebrates the variety of human actions, it avoids stating categorically that all humans are basically good or basically sinful.

Teacher role/learning styles   As stated earlier, the teacher is like an *investment counselor*. That means you would have a wide range of experiences and should be able to guide students into making the wisest choices considering their potential.

The broker does not function haphazardly but systematically. You would not only arrange for investments to be made, but you would continuously help students assess their yields. Compared with the other approaches, this one is most similar to the action approach, although it does not require quite as much "active" participation.

I have found five general arenas of life which appear to be most fruitful as constellations around which values education can be organized. These include feelings as well as cognitive activities, private concepts as well as attitudes to be expressed in public.

Values investment encourages deep student involvement, and it favors those teaching styles which Olson documented were most effective

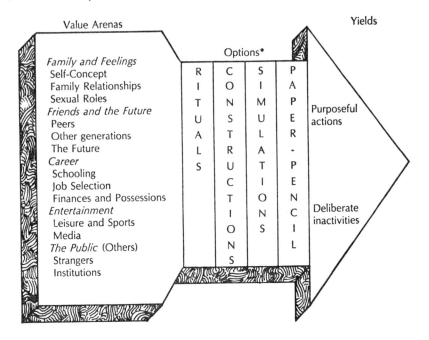

Value Arenas

Options*

Yields

Family and Feelings					
Self-Concept	R	C	S	P	
Family Relationships	I	O	I	A	
Sexual Roles	T	N	M	P	
Friends and the Future	U	S	U	E	Purposeful actions
Peers	A	T	L	R	
Other generations	L	R	A	-	
The Future	S	U	T	P	
Career		C	I	E	
Schooling		T	O	N	
Job Selection		I	N	C	Deliberate inactivities
Finances and Possessions		O	S	I	
Entertainment		N		L	
Leisure and Sports		S			
Media					
The Public (Others)					
Strangers					
Institutions					

* Rituals: Ceremonies, walk-throughs, field trips, laws, humor.
Constructions: Model building, film making, artistic projects.
Simulations: Dilemmas, games, role playing.
Paper-pencil: Research papers, diaries and biographies, value sheets, standardized tests, scales.

Figure 2–6   *The "Yield" Model of Values Investment*

if the teacher wishes to enhance creativity, interpersonal regard, individualization, and group activity.[39]

The favored strategies of values investment require more than simple responses. Some typical examples include: the analysis of a wedding ceremony (ritual); the drawing of a car of the future (construction); participation in "Win as Much as You Can" (simulation); and reports on the youth of famous Americans (paper-pencil instruments).

This approach stresses that it is necessary to have the students *investing* something of themselves—either in planning, carrying out (through spending time or even money), or declaring their decisions.

Theorists　The educational theorists who have influenced me include Phenix, *Realms of Meaning* and Buber, *Between Man and Man*. I have accepted a developmental view of the learning of values, as generally seen in the work of Erikson. The techniques of Raths, Harmin, and Simon have also affected the way I approach values education. [40]

Activity　"Your Feelings about School."

You have been a "veteran" of many years in school. Have you ever tried to express in some concrete way your feelings about it? Try to now.

Perhaps you are conditioned to write something down. Postpone that for now. Rather, to help focus your feelings, come up with some nonverbal symbol of your relationship to school. You might draw or paint a picture of the sun ("it gives me a warm feeling"). Or make a collage of magazine pictures ("a kaleidoscope of positive and negative messages") or construct a model ("here's a jail—I was hemmed in").

Value identification:　"Your Feelings About School."

Activity:　The participant expresses, through a nonverbal symbol, his or her feelings about school or some other institution.

Learning aids:　A take-home assignment, to allow for individual tastes.

Unit interaction:　Members of the group display their symbols, and discuss their meanings. Questions for discussion: Generally, are there more positive than negative comments made? Ask individuals, especially those who revealed some "extreme" like or dislike of schools.

Evaluation:　Personal report. This is very effective at the beginning of a school term. It can be used at the end of the quarter, and students are encouraged to see if they would use the same symbol again to describe their feelings about school.

Suggestions:　An alternative is to ask students what kinds of music they identify with when they think of schools. Or they could draw an impression of the teacher they most remember.

This profile indicates the *dominant* characteristics of each approach. In no way should it be viewed as totally inclusive.

Approach	Teaching style	Definition of value	Theory of valuing
Analysis	challenger (detective)	benefits standards process	training modeling cognitive dissonance
Moral reasoning	arranger questioner	universal truths valuing process	training
Transmission	model (gold star, picture perfect)	universal truths needs standards	modeling behavior modification
Integration	accepter (wise owl)	needs universal truths	behavior modification modeling goal setting
Values clarification	sharer (clarifier)	benefits standards valuing process	cognitive dissonance behavior patterns
Action	investigator (wise owl)	standards benefits needs	training cognitive dissonance
Evocation	stimulator (clarifier)	universal truths	training behavior patterns
Union	harmonizer (clarifier)	universal truths valuing process	training modeling
Investment	broker (travel agent)	standards valuing process needs	training goal setting cognitive dissonance

Table 2-1   *Profile of Nine Values Education Approaches*

SUMMARY

Now that you have finished an examination of various definitions of values and theories of valuing and have applied them to nine possible approaches to values education, you may wish to return to the pretest and compare your feelings then and now. Are you still loyal to one approach? Do you prefer to try out several? If you feel you still need more information before you can answer these questions, read chapter 3.

Notes

1. C. Ellis Nelson, ed., *Conscience* (New York: Newman, 1973). Key writers in theology and psychology discuss the ramifications of this position.

2. Sigmund Freud, *The Future of an Illusion* (New York: Anchor Books, 1961; first published 1927); Abraham Maslow, *Motivation and Personality* (New York: Harper, 1954); Erich Fromm, *Man for Himself: An Inquiry into the Psychology of Ethics* (New York: Holt, 1947).

3. Zelda Blanchette, et al., *The Human Value Series* (Austin, Tex.: Steck-Vaughn Company, 1970).

4. Nicolas Rescher, *Introduction to Value Theory* (Englewood Cliffs, N.J.: Prentice-Hall, 1969), p. 2.

5. Robert Hogan, "Moral Conduct and Moral Character: A Psychological Perspective," *Psychological Bulletin* 79, no. 4 (April 1973): pp. 217–30.

6. Louis Raths, Merrill Harmin, and Sidney Simon, *Values and Teaching* (Columbus, Ohio: Charles E. Merrill, 1966), pp. 29–30.

7. Howard Kirschenbaum, "Beyond Values Clarification," in Sidney Simon and Howard Kirschenbaum, eds., *Readings in Values Clarification* (Minneapolis: Winston Press, 1974), p. 92–110.

8. The work of Fishbein and Raven (1962) is cited by Milton Rokeach, *Beliefs, Attitudes and Values* (San Francisco: Jossey-Bass, 1968). For further comments see M. Fishbein, "Attitude and the Prediction of Behavior," in M. Fishbein (ed.), *Readings in Attitude Theory and Measurement* (New York: Wiley, 1967).

9. Rokeach, *Beliefs*, p. 2.

10. D. Krech, R. S. Crutchfield, and E. L. Ballachey, *Individual in Society* (New York: McGraw-Hill, 1962); as cited by Rokeach, *Beliefs*, p. 113.

11. Rokeach, *Beliefs*, p. 112.

12. Rokeach, *Beliefs*, p. 160.

13. The approach advocated by the *Skills for Ethical Action* course is similar to mine. The steps are: (1) value naming—students identify and rank what is important to them; (2) get action ideas—students generate ideas for specific personal actions that might further their values; (3) check workability—students ensure that the action ideas are possible to carry out now; (4) consider the consequences to self—students weigh potential benefits or harm to themselves from the possible action(s); (5) consider the consequences to others—students weigh potential benefit or harm to others from the possible action(s); (6) act—students commit themselves to an action and carry it out; (7) reflect—students evaluate the effect of the action on themselves and others and reexamine the initial value(s). Research for Better Schools, Inc., Philadelphia, Pennsylvania, produced this junior-high course.

14. *Life Magazine*, "Launching Healthy Children" (December 17, 1971). A special supplement.

15. Erik H. Erikson, *Childhood and Society* (New York: Norton, 1950; 2nd ed., 1963), pp. 247–74. For a discussion of peer influence, see D. Dorr and S. Fey, "Relative Power of Symbolic Adult and Peer Models, in the Modification of Children's Moral Choice Behavior," *Journal of Personality and Social Psychology* 29 (March 1974), pp. 335–41.

16. Hogan, "Moral Conduct," pp. 225–30. E. Goffman, *The Presentation of Self in Everyday Life* (Garden City, N.Y.: Doubleday, 1959).

17. Lawrence Kohlberg, "The Cognitive-Developmental Approach to Moral Education, *Phi Delta Kappan* 56, no. 10 (June 1975), pp. 670–77. Also Kohlberg, *Development and Behavior* (New York: Holt, 1976). Also R. F. Peck and Robert J. Havighurst, *The Psychology of Character Development* (New York: Wiley, 1960), and R. B. Perry, *Realms of Value* (Cambridge, Mass.: Harvard University Press, 1954).

18. Modified from Lawrence Kohlberg, "Understanding the Hidden Curriculum,"

Learning 1, no. 2 (December 1972), pp. 10–14. See also Beverly A. Mattox, *Getting It Together* (San Diego: Pennant Press, 1975), for dilemmas for the classroom based on Kohlberg's approach.

19. John D. Krumboltz and Helen B. Krumboltz, *Changing Children's Behavior* (Englewood Cliffs, N.J.: Prentice-Hall, 1972). Also Sven Lindskold, et al., "Developmental Aspects of Positive Inducements," *Developmental Psychology* 3, no. 3 (1970), pp. 277–84.

20. B. F. Skinner, *The Technology of Teaching* (New York: Appleton-Century-Crofts, 1968). Irwin G. Sarason, et al., eds., *Reinforcing Productive Classroom Behavior* (New York: Behavioral Publications, 1972). Earl White and Hazel I. Smith, *A Guide to Behavior Modification: A Classroom Teacher's Handbook* (Palo Alto, Calif.: Peak Publications, 1972).

21. L. Festinger, *A Theory of Cognitive Dissonance* (Stanford: Stanford University Press, 1957). Milton Rokeach, "Persuasion That Persists," *Psychology Today* 5, no. 4 (September 1971), pp. 68–71, 92.

22. William Glasser, *Schools Without Failure* (New York: Harper, 1969).

23. Abraham Maslow, ed., *New Knowledge in Human Values* (New York: Harper, 1959). Frank Goble, *The Third Force* (New York: Grossman Press, 1970; 2nd ed., Pocket Books, 1971).

24. This is also called *self-perception research*. See B. Calder and M. Ross, "Attitude and Behavior," 1973 booklet available from General Learning Press, 250 James Street, Morristown, New Jersey.

25. Reprinted by permission of the Social Science Education Consortium from Superka, Douglas, et al., *Values Education Sourcebook* (Boulder, Col.: Social Science Education Consortium, 1976). For a briefer treatment of the scope of values education, see Douglas Superka, "Approaches to Values Education," Social Science Education Consortium *Newsletter* (November 1974). For journal articles related to this topic, consult such sources as *Educational Theory*, which may be ordered from the Education Building, University of Illinois, Urbana, Illinois. For a general reader on attitude theory, see Samuel Himmelfarb and Alice Eagly, eds., *Readings in Attitude Change* (New York: Wiley, 1974).

26. Albert Ellis, *Reason and Emotion in Psychotherapy* (New York: Lyle Stuart, 1962). George A. Kelly, *The Psychology of Personal Constructs* (New York: Norton, 1955). Superka, *Sourcebook*, pp. 55–57.

27. James A. Banks, *Teaching Strategies for the Social Studies: Inquiry, Valuing, Decision-Making* (Reading, Mass.: Addison-Wesley, 1973).

28. Michael Scriven, *Primary Philosophy* (New York: McGraw-Hill, 1966), and "Cognitive Moral Education," *Kappan* 56, no. 10 (June 1975), pp. 689–94. Stephen C. Pepper, *The Sources of Value* (Berkeley, Calif.: University of California Press, 1958). Rollo Handy, *Value Theory and the Behavioral Sciences* (Springfield, Ill.: Thomas, 1969).

29. Jean Piaget, *The Moral Judgment of the Child* (New York: Collier, 1962; 1st ed., 1932). Clive Beck, ed., *Moral Education* (Ontario: University of Toronto Press, 1971). Jane Loevinger, et al., *Measuring Ego Development, I and II* (San Francisco: Jossey-Bass, 1970). Superka, *Sourcebook*, pp. 31–36.

30. W. Ray Rucker, Clyde V. Arnspiger, and Arthur J. Brodbeck, *Human Values in Education* (Dubuque, Iowa: Kendall/Hunt, 1969). Superka, *Sourcebook*, pp. 7–12.

31. Talcott Parsons, *The Social System* (Glencoe, Ill.: The Free Press, 1951). Abraham Maslow, *Toward a Psychology of Being* (Princeton, N.J.: Van Nostrand, 1962). Robert R. Sears, et al., *Patterns of Child Rearing* (Evanston, Ill.: Row, Peterson, 1957).

32. Carl Rogers, *Freedom to Learn* (Columbus, Ohio: Merrill, 1969). Haim Ginott, *Between Parent and Child: New Solutions to Old Problems* (New York: Macmillan, 1967). Thomas Harris, *I'm OK, You're OK* (New York: Avon Books, 1973; 1st ed., 1967). Thomas Gordon, *Parent Effectiveness Training (P.E.T.)* (New York: Wyden, 1970).

33. John Dewey, *Experience and Education* (New York: Macmillan, 1938), and *Moral Principles in Education* (New York: Philosophical Library, 1959). Raths, Harmin, and Simon, *Values in Teaching*. Sidney Simon, *Meeting Yourself Halfway* (Niles, Ill.: Argus

Communications, 1974). Fannie Shaftel and George Shaftel, *Values in Action* (New York: Holt, 1970).

34. Herbert Blumer, *Symbolic Interactionism: Perspective and Method* (Englewood Cliffs, N.J.: Prentice-Hall, 1969). Morris L. Bigge, *Positive Relativism: An Emergent Educational Philosophy* (New York: Harper, 1971). Harry S. Sullivan, *The Interpersonal Theory of Psychiatry* (New York: Norton, 1953).

35. Superka, *Newsletter.* p. 4.

36. Robert E. Samples, "Value Prejudice: Toward a Personal Awareness," *Media and Methods* 11 (September 1974), pp. 14–18, 49–52.

37. Arthur W. Combs and Donald Snygg, *Individual Behavior: A Perceptual Approach* (New York: Harper, 1949). Carl A. Whitaker and Thomas P. Malone, *The Roots of Psychotherapy* (New York: Blakiston, 1953). Richard M. Jones, *Fantasy and Feeling in Education* (New York: Harper, 1968). Weinstein and Fantini, *Toward Humanistic Education.*

38. Paul Tillich, *The Courage to Be* (New Haven: Yale University Press, 1952). Alan W. Watts, *The Book: On the Taboo Against Knowing Who You Are* (New York: Collier, 1967). Francis Driscoll, "TM as a Secondary School Subject," *Kappan* 54, no. 4 (December 1972), pp. 236–37.

39. Martin N. Olson, "Ways to Achieve Quality in School Classrooms: Some Definite Answers," *Phi Delta Kappan* 33, no. 1 (September 1971), pp. 63–65.

40. Philip Phenix, *Realms of Meaning* (New York: McGraw-Hill, 1964).

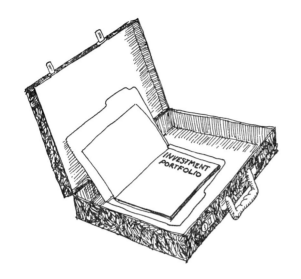

THE
PORTFOLIO

Part two, "The Portfolio," concentrates upon the many available curricular materials. Chapter 3 highlights the curriculum sets related to the nine approaches. In addition to describing the sets, the chapter provides some clues to how to select the best materials for your particular situation.

Chapter 4 focuses on media which can be used in values education. Because so many of the media listed could be adapted to several approaches, Chapter 4 is organized not around the nine approaches, but around media types.

Curriculum

One theme of this book is that you and I are valuable. We are valuable because we are unique, each composed of a myriad of characteristics, including whims and talents.

Moreover, we are value-able, because we must make choices as we live, work, and play in our daily lives. All of us continually make priority decisions about what we choose to do, where we shall go, what we want to acquire, and what we will not do.

As a teacher and values educator, one of your fundamental choices will be the curriculum you select to use with your class. Chapter 2 offered a questionnaire to help you determine where you stand on values education. It might be helpful to review your position again.

Before we turn to specific curricula, I should reveal some of *my* personal beliefs. I believe that every teacher should "customize" the curriculum for the students' needs. This is easier said than done, and therefore many teachers will have to rely upon formal materials. What I want to encourage, then, is that you develop enough confidence in what you are doing that you can adapt special activities and media to your basic curriculum.

You will probably be in one of the following four stances relative to the choosing of curriculum.

1. You are free to select any curriculum you want, and budget is not an important consideration.

2. You are free to select curriculum, but budget is very important.

3. You are either part of a curriculum committee or in some advisory role in the selection of instructional materials.

4. You are given materials which you have to teach.

Regardless of the posture in which you may find yourself, this chapter should help you make the best decision for your situation.

The chapter will try to do more than give you a look at curriculum sets. It should help you appraise your own teaching style, provide you with criteria to evaluate all types of curricula, and suggest some general guidelines for justifying sensitive educational topics to concerned students, parents, patrons, and fellow educators. Also, you will be given the names and addresses of organizations involved in values education which can offer you continuing help.

GENERAL AIDS

There are so many curriculum materials now that it is virtually impossible to keep up with them. There are, however, several references which can provide a framework for approaching the evaluation of values materials.

Without doubt, the best resource today for systematically reviewing the variety of materials in values education is Douglas Superka, et. al., *Values Education Sourcebook.*[1] This reference book should be available in every school district for those who wish to consider values education, because it provides an in-depth look at the conceptual approaches we shall be discussing. It analyzes materials and has an extensive bibliography. Since in this chapter we are concentrating upon curriculum sets, I will not single out individual textbooks which have value themes. A number of other sources are available if you wish to explore such topics as determining moral goals and establishing a learning environment for values education.[2]

Two good articles about the curricular importance of values education and teaching methodology for this area are Alpern, "Curriculum Significance of the Affective Domain" and Rembert, "Teaching about Values."[3]

Journals

The following periodicals offer articles which relate to the affective domain on a regular basis.

Educational Theory, a philosophical and theoretical publication produced by the University of Illinois.

The Humanist, published by Hoffman Printing Company, 923 Kensington Avenue, Buffalo, New York, 14215.

Journal of Humanistic Psychology, from the Association for Humanistic Psychology, 416 Hoffman Street, San Francisco, California, 94114.

Journal of Moral Education, published by Pergamon Press. Appears approximately three times a year. Related to the Farmington Trust Research Unit in Great Britain.

Learning, although designed for elementary teachers, has provocative articles on values education which will be of interest to many. Published by Education Today Co., 530 University Avenue, Palo Alto, California 94301.

Moral Education Forum, 221 E. 72nd Street, New York, New York, 10021, is a recent publication which focuses on the developmental approach.

Phi Delta Kappan, a leading "issues of education" journal which had a special issue on moral education in June, 1975.

Religious Education, published by the Religious Education Association, 409 Prospect Street, New Haven, Connecticut, 06510.

Theory into Practice, which devoted its October, 1975, issue to moral education.

Most university libraries also have available the Educational Resources Information Center (ERIC) system. ERIC lists new research findings on values education in abstract format. The reports selected for inclusion include recent journal articles, summaries of funded projects, and papers given at national conferences. Most libraries also have the *Educational Index,* which cites current articles in journals for professional educators.

Organizations

The following organizations are either deeply committed to curriculum development or teacher training in the area of values education.

Achievement Motivation Program (111 East Wacker Drive, Suite 510, Chicago, Illinois 60601). Supported by the Stone Foundation, this organization has developed several curriculum sets which are distributed by the Encyclopedia Brittanica Company. AMP also organizes teacher-training programs which focus on goal setting.

American Institute for Character Education (P. O. Box 12617, San Antonio, Texas 78212). Under a Lilly Endowment grant, this group developed the Character Education Project. Currently it is focusing on research into development of character and on character education training.

Association of Moral Development in Education (Harvard University, Cambridge, Massachusetts 02138). Related to the Kohlberg approach, this agency does some research for that approach and serves as a clearinghouse for materials.

Disseminators of Knowledge (71 Radcliffe Road, Buffalo, New York 14214). This firm produces affective educational materials.

Essentia (P. O. Box 129, Tiburon, California 94920). A training center for those who are drawn to the evocation approach.

National Humanistic Education Center (110 Spring St., Saratoga Springs, New York 12866). Directed by Howard Kirschenbaum, this organization is the focal point for the Values Clarification Trainers Network.

Nebraska Human Resources Research Foundation (501 Building, University of Nebraska, Lincoln, Nebraska 68508). This organization trains teachers to work with young children through human relations techniques.

Pennant Educational Materials (4680 Canyon Road, San Diego, California 92120). Primarily a clearinghouse for curriculum materials, especially related to the transmission, moral reasoning, and values clarification approaches, it also publishes some materials.

PERSC. (Public Education Religion Studies Center, Wright State University, Dayton, Ohio 45431). This agency serves as a clearinghouse and policy-making organization for those interested in teaching about religion in public schools.

Research for Better Schools, Inc. (Suite 1700/1700 Market Street, Philadelphia, Pennsylvania 19103). This nonprofit, private organization is trying to bring various approaches together for joint projects. It has also developed its own approach to values education with a curriculum at the junior high level.

Social Science Education Consortium (855 Broadway, Boulder, Colorado 80302). Working with social science teachers, and sponsored largely by federal funds, this group has produced several major works on values-related materials (by Superka).

Value Education Consultants Clearinghouse (P. O. Box 947, Campbell, California 95008). This firm organizes workshops for teachers. They use the format of Lasswell and Rucker.

Values Education Center (2468 Glenwood School Drive, Burlington, Ontario, Canada L7L, 1C4). Dr. John R. Meyer is Director of a project which has been doing classroom assessment and in-service professional development since 1973.

This list is just a sampling of organizations which wish to share their interest in values education. You should be on the lookout for regional groups in your area which form a local information network to meet and discuss their activities.

Value Activity: Your Teaching Style

All of the curriculum approaches which will be described seem geared to certain teaching styles more than others. Why not check out whether your teaching style is characteristic of your instruction?

In the blanks below, next to each label, enter first the letter *A* (actual) or the letter *P* (prefer), depending on whether you actually do use that style or would prefer to use that style. After the letter add the percentage of time you believe you actually teach or would like to teach in that manner. Example: <u>A–40%</u>   <u>P–20%</u> Exposition. Each term is defined below.

_____   Exposition

_____   Recitation

_____   Guided discussion
            (leading questions)

_____   Guided discussion
            (open-ended questions)

_____   Role play/simulation

_____   Discovery

_____   Community involvement

_____   Constructions

Exposition: A setting forth of facts, ideas, and so on by a teacher, guest speaker, textbook, film, or other media. It is content-oriented, with the goal being memorization and recall of information. Other forms include giving directions and setting forth a procedure.

Recitation: This is a companion of exposition. After the lecture, film, or reading, the students are asked questions which recall information. Recitation is also used for checking on comprehension of theories or data presented.

Guided discussion, leading questions: Sample activities include analyzing data, drawing inferences, applying conceptual models, and, given criteria, evaluating a behavior. Through the discussion and leading questions the teacher arranges data and develops inquiry skills.

Guided discussion, open-ended questions: This method is likely to be used in instructional sequences involving matters of value and personal commitment, matters of meaning and interpretation, and areas which have alternative explanations. The teacher's goal is to elicit a student conclusion and probe the reasoning, both factual and valuative, to foster the students' personal awareness and inquiry ability.

Role-playing/simulation: In both these techniques, the teacher arranges a situation and then acts as an observer. Conflict of interests is usually a key ingredient. One goal is to encourage participants to share their feelings and values. These methods can be used to teach relationships of political and social systems.

Discovery: The teacher presents an initial stimulus, such as an artifact, a problem and data, or a perplexing visual display, and withdraws from the discussion. Students then pose questions, suggest hypotheses, challenge them, and arrive at conclusions.

Community involvement: Visits to museums, talks with community leaders, attending celebrations and services, and investigating a variety of neighborhood activities are samples of involvement.

Constructions: Students build models of things they want to have or illustrate ways in which they would alter some part of their world, personal or social.

Value identification: "Teaching Styles." (Modified from an activity originally developed by the Religion Social Studies Curriculum Project, Tallahassee, Florida).[4]

Activity: After completion of survey, participants will analyze their own teaching styles.

Learning aids: Handout.

Unit interaction: If done in a group, allow thirty minutes for completion of survey. Questions used for discussion are given in Evaluation section.

Evaluation: Discussion of survey results, to be aided by these questions: Recall the most successful methods which you have used in the past. What were they? What does the difference between your actual and preferred choices tell you?

Suggestions: A somewhat similar activity is found in Richard L. Curwin and Barbara S. Fuhrmann, *Discovering Your Teaching Self: Humanistic Approaches to Effective Teaching.*[5]

CHOOSING AND DEFENDING VALUES CURRICULA

Choosing Curricula

Superka and his associates have developed an exercise to help you choose from among various sets of values education materials.[6] They suggest you choose from their list of eighteen key questions the nine which seem most important to you. Place an asterisk beside each of those nine questions. Next, divide these questions into three groups by placing a "1" beside the three questions of greatest importance, a "2" beside those of secondary importance, and a "3" beside those of least importance. You should have some idea then of what is most important to you as you choose or advise others to choose values materials.

_____ Is the approach embodied in the materials similar to the approach you believe is the best?

_____ Do the rationale and objectives fit your own?

_____ Is the reading level appropriate to your students?

_____ Is there little or no racial or ethnic bias and sterotyping in the materials?

_____ Is there little or no sexual bias and stereotyping in the materials?

_____ Is special teacher training required to use the materials? If so, is it provided?

_____ Will obtaining school or community acceptance for using the materials be a problem?

_____ Is the time sequence of materials suited to your needs?

_____ Will the content and activities involve and interest your students?

_____ Do the materials emphasize the process of valuing instead of the content?

_____ Do the materials stress personal as well as social value questions?

_____ Do the materials use a variety of teaching methods and learning activities?

_____ Does the teacher's guide (if provided) offer guidelines for applying the procedures or strategies?

_____ Are the rights of learners to withhold personal information protected?

_____ Are specific evaluation procedures or instruments provided to determine student growth?

_____ Have the materials been and do they continue to be field-tested or learner-verified?

_____ Do the materials contain carefully planned, detailed lessons, or are they basically a resource that teachers can use any way they see fit?

_____ (Your own questions):

When you mark your top three choices, ask yourself if they place you consistently within one of the nine approaches.

Defending Values Curricula

Selecting the best values curriculum for your situation is a major step. Before you actually begin using it, you should also think through another dimension of values education. What will you do about criticisms of the program from people who are upset by it?

What if a student quietly informed you that an announced values activity on environmental pollution would be embarrassing because his father owns a factory which has been cited for violations? What would you say to a parent who called to complain that a proposed discussion would contradict the family's religious convictions? How would you respond if a fellow teacher or administrator accused you of imposing your values on students when your class discussed certain playground behaviors? What would you say if a concerned citizen protested that you are doing too much when your class begins a study of rental conditions in your community?

Are there some general guidelines you might develop to help you cope with situations similar to these? I think so.

Student-Related Policies

1. A climate of acceptance.   Most values education programs are built upon a classroom climate which encourages open discussion by all participants. By word and action you need to show clearly that you wish to have a trusting, truthful relationship established. How can that be done?

Members of the class have to believe that they are free to share their opinions without fear of put-down or reprisal. To develop this spirit you'll have to demonstrate that a variety of alternatives can be discussed.

Realistically, you face the problem of peer pressure and subtle teacher clues about what are acceptable views and behaviors. Perhaps you should have a discussion with your class about the power of the majority. De Tocqueville, the colonial French visitor to the United States, observed the democratic process and noted that one of its problems would be the "tyranny of the majority."

2. Objective discussions.   One goal for classroom interaction can be objective discussions. Being objective does not have to mean "devoid of feelings." Philip Phenix suggests that being objective should mean that we vigorously attempt to "get inside the heads and hearts" of the advocates of the points of view that we are debating, reflecting as accurately and as persuasively as we can their feelings and beliefs.[7]

3. Grading. There is close to unanimous acceptance among values educators that grading value strategies will doom them. The pressure of the grade forces students to play the "what does the teacher want" game.

4. Participation not required. You should make some decision about protecting individuals who are sensitive on certain topics. The values clarification approach has a flat policy that anyone can "pass" on any activity. But this policy can also cause difficulties. With one group I have worked with, this policy of passing was being actively used by one member. Several other participants were upset because they believed that it was putting a damper on the discussion. To counter this, you have to let students know that they all benefit more when they all share, but that you will respect the "pass" policy.

5. Rules. Your educational situation may require you to develop other rules, which should be made clear. A. J. Grainger, a teacher in Great Britain, wanted to foster a moral education program and wished to develop a time when the class would meet in a circle. Grainger believed these rules were essential:

1. Damage must not be done to school or personal property.
2. There must be no excessive noise.
3. Acting in such a way as to cause physical harm is forbidden.
4. The meeting must stop if anyone enters the room and normal respect must be shown to teachers or children coming in on school business, etc. . . .[8]

The group understood the rules and had spirited discussions.

General Policies
Outside the classroom you should be prepared for questions raised by the inquiring and the irate alike.

1. Philosophy. You're on the right track when you have a clear understanding of the philosophy of your school system, of your own approach, and of the curriculum you adopt.

2. Objections policy. Do you know the procedures for filing and responding to complaints? Some educational agencies have developed their own, some follow suggestions of the American Library Association or the National Council of Teachers of English, and some don't have any policy.

3. Locate the real cause.   When individuals protest either a curriculum set, book, or a practice, try to find out what the real objective is. In one Western state, it was reported that protests were raised against the book *Bless the Beasts and Children* because of the foul language. When the school textbook committee agreed to change the language, the protester finally admitted that it was not the language that bothered him—it was the "message" he received, that the book advocated gun control!

4. Admitting a mistake.   Be prepared to admit that within a curriculum set there may be an activity or story which is inappropriate for the age or situation of the group you are working with. There can be legitimate objections.

5. The issue of action.   Perhaps the major question here is the question of action. A number of values approaches indicate that values require action. How willing are you to have your students become really active? Do you want them writing letters to editors? Investigating "problems" in the community? Challenging school policies? You might find it helpful to discuss with your class general rules regarding the age-old dilemma of trying to work within a system to improve it, or finding it is too firmly established to change, and leaving.[9]

SELECTING A
VALUES CURRICULUM

As indicated earlier, the *Values Education Sourcebook* is the best single tool for analyzing the curriculum sets in values education. The remainder of this chapter highlights the various approaches and briefly notes some curriculum sets.

There are minor differences in the typologies drawn by Superka and those which I use. I have divided his inculcation approach into the transmission and integration approaches, for there are differences between those sets which primarily promote such social goals as patriotism and loyalty and good citizenship (i.e., transmission) and those that primarily stress building self-concept, becoming more aware of feelings, and building skills in problem-solving (i.e., integration).

All approaches use some inculcation. That is, each approach does have certain traits and values which it advocates. Even those which claim to be chiefly concerned about the valuing process or analytical skills propose that students will be tolerant of other viewpoints and that they will be fair in giving others a chance to speak. Almost all approaches favor a rational lifestyle. Even teachers of the supposedly noninculcating approaches are supposed to invite emulation.

Each of the nine approaches will be reviewed in the following format: purposes, teacher models, methods, and sample activity. Then brief descriptions of teacher materials and a list of curriculum sets will be provided. Mailing addresses of the publishers can be found in Appendix B.

The review of each approach will close with an assessment, using a modification of the **V-A-L-U-E-S** system. The first category will be **Value** concepts. If the curriculum sets in an approach maintain consistency with its stated purposes, they will be rated high. For example, if the analysis approach teacher guides continually provide methods which do ask the instructors to build logical skills and research potential for their students, they would be rated high. If the guides wandered into evocation activities and union strategies, they would be rated low.

The assessment will next reflect my opinion on the **Activities** of the sets. Are the activities or objectives clearly stated? Within sets, are the objectives organized coherently? If the integration approach is found to be halfway between clearly stated objectives and muddy intentions, it would be rated medium.

Are there a variety of **Learning aids?** Should the action activities be found to be highly repititious, they would be rated low. Is there a blend of print and media, active as well as quiet strategies, and individual as well as group games? If the answer is yes, the approach would be rated high.

How adequate are the descriptions of the **Unit interactions** or class projects? Is there evidence indicating students respond enthusiastically to the typical formats of the strategies?

Do the sets offer meaningful techniques for **Evaluation?** Is there a tendency, for example, for the transmission approach to rely on observation techniques? Does the evocation approach resist formal measurement? If so, it would be rated low.

The **Suggestion** category is used to indicate the degree of flexibility with each approach. Do the writers typically offer alternative activities? Are the strategies tightly structured, or easy to modify?

As you've probably noted, I use the terms "high," "medium," and "low" on a continuum of my agreement or disagreement with the questions raised. Because of the diversity within certain approaches, it will be impossible to make this kind of overall evaluation.

Remember, this is *my* rating. A high or low rating is in itself not a sign of strength or weakness. The final assessment will be up to you, as you decide whether you prefer a set which is highly organized or one that is informal.

Values Analysis

Purposes: To help students think logically and use scientific investigation to decide value issues and questions; to provide activities which will build students' skills in using rational, analytical processes in interrelating and conceptualizing their values.

Teacher model: The teacher has two roles: a guide to resources, and the devil's advocate for positions the students have developed.

Methods: A favorite instrument would be structured rational discussion that demands application of reasons as well as evidence. The steps in the process would include gathering evidence, testing principles, analyzing analogous cases, debating, and doing more research.

Sample activities: At the elementary level, students would build data banks of facts on social issues, develop scenarios of incidents in history ("Why did President X decide to . . . and was that the right decision?"), role play, and gather information through telephone interviews or visits with leading figures in the community.

A typical secondary activity would be making up the evidence cards, as shown in chapter 2. Studies of other cultures, inquiry activities, and collections of readings would be used.

Resources: For the teacher, these sources would give an adequate introduction to the theory of values analysis as well as sample activities:

Lawrence Metcalf, *Values Education: Rationale, Strategies, Procedures* (Washington, D.C.: National Council for Social Studies Yearbook, 1971), suitable for K–12 teachers.

Jack Fraenkel, *Teaching Students to Think and Value* (Englewood Cliffs, N.J.: Prentice-Hall, 1973).

John V. Michaelis, *Social Studies for Children in a Democracy* (Englewood Cliffs, N.J.: Prentice-Hall, 1973).

Curriculum sets include:

Donald Oliver and Fred Newman, *Public Issues Series* (Columbus, Ohio: Xerox, 1967–74), grades 9–12. The Harvard Social Studies Series uses an historical framework and strategies including dialogues, case studies, and lectures.

James Shaver and A. Guy Larkins, *Analysis of Public Issues Program* (Boston: Houghton-Mifflin, 1973), grades 9–12.

David L. Bender and Gary E. McCuen, *Opposing Viewpoints Series* (Anoka, Mn.: Greenhaven Press, 1971–74), grades 8–12. Centers on values of American foreign policy through the use of simulation gaming, exercises which separate fact from opinion, and confrontation situations. Has a unit on "The Problem of Death," which includes topics such as suicide, abortion, and capital punishment.

Mary C. Durkin and Anthony H. McNaughton, *The Taba Program in Social Science* (Reading, Mass.: Addison-Wesley, 1972–74), grades K–7. Concentrates upon such processes as listing, labeling, and comparing, which could be helpful in the clarifying process.

Paul Brandwein, *The Social Sciences: Concepts and Values* (New York: Harcourt, 1970–75), grades K–8. The set emphasizes inquiry skills and gathering of evidence.

Jack Nelson, *American Values Series: Challenges and Choices* (Rochelle Park, N.J.: Hayden, 1974–75), grades 9–12. Titles include "The Rights of Women" and "The Environment."

Vincent Ryan Ruggiero, *The Moral Imperative* (Alfred Publishing, 1973), grades 11–12. Themes in this set are moral and ethical decision making. One goal is to build cultural appreciation.

Harold Berlak and Timothy R. Tomlinson, *Peoples/Choices/Decisions* (New York: Random House, 1973), grades 4–6. Using a number of readings, discussions, and role-playing situations as well as media, it frequently asks students to take a position and defend it. Titles include "A Village Family" and "One City Neighborhood."

Vincent Rogers, *The Values and Decisions Series* (Columbus, Ohio: Xerox, 1972–74), grades 7–12. Many of the situations used are political, including descriptions of Vietnam.

Assessment of values analysis:

Value concepts: High. Most sets show a marked concern for rational choices and consistently stress scientific methodology.

Activities: High to medium. Individual lessons are not always stated with behavioral objectives.

Learning aids: Medium. Some variety, but most are research-related and highly verbal.

Unit interaction: Varies considerably. Generally comments on class organization and follow-through procedures are explained. A few sets seem to assume you will know what to do.

Evaluation: Medium to low. Surprisingly weak, considering the high-level structure elsewhere.

Suggestions: Medium. Rather rigid in expectations of what is to be done. There is usually a close relationship to subject matter.

Moral Reasoning

Purposes: To help students develop more complex moral-reasoning patterns. Like the values analysis system, moral reasoning places a high priority on cognitive processes, urging students to discuss the reasons for their value choices and positions. Unlike some other approaches, it is not just for the purpose of sharing, but with the intent that students may experience other reasoning systems and perhaps advance their own.

Teacher model: The teacher is an arranger who provides the dilemma stories and "sets up" the group discussion. Within the group discussion, the teacher functions as a "prober" who encourages members to reason through all possible solutions to the dilemma.

Methods: The typical technique is a moral dilemma episode with a small group discussion which is relatively structured and argumentive.

Sample activities: At the elementary level dilemma stories or picture cards pose a situation to be solved. Role plays and conflict situations on tape or filmstrip are used frequently at the secondary level.

Resources:

Beverly A. Mattox, *Getting It Together* (San Diego: Pennant, 1975), grades K–12. Provides a number of dilemmas based on the Kohlberg model. In addition to the dilemmas, she offers suggestions for designing your own.

Ron Galbraith and Thomas M. Jones, *Moral Reasoning* (Anoka, Mn.: Greenhaven Press, 1976). Somewhat more theoretical than Mattox.

Edmund V. Sullivan, *Moral Learning* (New York: Paulist Press, 1975). Discusses research done on the Kohlberg model.

John Wilson, *Practical Methods of Moral Education* (London: Heinemann Educational Books, 1972). Similar to, but not based on, Kohlberg.

There are only a few curriculum sets which have adopted this approach. Several mentioned below could be crosslisted as media materials.

Lawrence Kohlberg and Robert Selman, *First Things: Values,* (Pleasant-ville, N.Y.: Guidance Associates, 1972), grades 1–5. A filmstrip set which asks the students to determine what is fair in a land of make-believe.

Edwin Fenton (ed.), *Holt Social Studies Curriculum* (New York: Holt, 1973), grades 9–12. A sample title is "Comparative Political Systems: An Inquiry Approach." Research for this set was done at the Carnegie-Mellon College. This particular set takes great pains in presenting the pros and cons of various governmental systems.

Alan Lockwood, *Moral Reasoning: The Value of Life* (Columbus, Ohio: Xerox, 1972), grades 9–12. The key question of this program is "What is the value of life (and) under what circumstances, if any, is it right to take a life?"

David Bender and Gary McCuen, *Photo Study Cards* (Anoka, Mn.: Greenhaven Press, 1974), grades 8–12. Photographs are used to discuss such questions as "Who are you?" "Who would you like to be?" "You and social responsibility. What is it?"

Assessment of moral reasoning:

Values concepts: Medium. Although Kohlberg's six stages are often referred to, a number of the sets do not clearly follow through in showing the relationships of the dilemmas to particular stages.

Activities: Medium to high. Objectives are stated fairly well.

Learning aids: Medium. Dilemmas are used almost to the exclusion of other means.

Unit interaction: Medium. Student interest is good on many activities, but instructions for developing various value themes are somewhat vague.

Evaluation: Medium to low. One of the difficulties of this approach has been its inability to get consistent findings from researchers.

Suggestions: Medium to low. The stories seem to carry the burden of instruction and typically few other options are suggested. Galbraith and Jones is an exception.

Transmission

Purposes: To instill or internalize certain desired values in the student. Typically they are social values such as nationalism and citizenship, respect for elders and authority, punctuality and courage.

Teacher model: The teacher serves as an agent for society by serving as a model of appropriate behavior. By setting up rules, the teacher serves as an authority figure.

Methods: Texts are frequently used, many with biographies. Guided discussion with leading questions is also a popular method. Games and simulations are less frequently tried. The teacher will also use positive and negative reinforcement, mocking, nagging, and providing incomplete or inaccurate data.

Sample activities: At the elementary level a number of sets use stories which have obvious moral implications. The favorite approach at the secondary level is the use of biography to learn how to live.

Resources:

Robert C. Hawley, *Human Values in the Classroom: Teaching for Personal and Social Growth* (Amherst, Mass.: Education Research Associates, 1973), grades K–12. A teacher's sourcebook.

Virginia Trevitt, *The American Heritage* (Santa Barbara, Calif.: McNally & Loftin, 1964), grades 7–9. A single text which uses many stories of America's forefathers. Guided discussions and questions are often suggested.

American Institute for Character Education, *Character Education Curriculum* (San Antonio: AICE, 1974), grades K–5. A list of fourteen values including honesty, truthfulness, helpfulness, and courage are taught through this material. It is highly organized by objectives and lists many suggestions for supplementary media.

Barbara Milbauer, et. al., *The Getting in Touch Series* (Stevensville, Mich.: Educational Services, 1973), grades 7–9. Uses an informal style and colorful art work to promote discussions on such topics as drug education.

Blanche A. Leonard, *Building Better Bridges with Ben* (Santa Monica, Calif.: Sunny Enterprises, 1974), grades 4–8. Benjamin Franklin's life and writings are used to discuss such virtues as frugality, sincerity, and humility. Students are encouraged to make a calendar like Franklin's and include comments on practicing the virtues Franklin promoted.

Zelda B. Blanchette, V. Clyde Arnspiger, James A. Brill, and W. Ray Rucker, *The Human Values Series* (Austin, Tex.: Steck-Vaughn, 1970, 1973), grades K–6. Posits that there are eight universal values, including wealth, affection, respect, well being, power, rectitude, skills, and enlightenment. Usually each story will focus on two of the values. Students are expected to become more proficient in identifying the eight values in the stories and then relating them to incidents in their own lives. A series of instruments have been created to test the inculcation of the eight values.

Joan Sayre, *Teaching Moral Values Through Behavioral Modification* (Danville, Ill.: Interstate, 1972), grades 3–5. Although Superka places this in a different category, I believe it belongs in the transmission approach because there are definite expectations that the students are expected to improve their values in the areas of prejudice, personal ethics, responsibility, and respect for authority.

Assessment of transmission:

Values concepts: High. Clear directions on the goals are typically stated.

Activities: High. Objectives are quite specific.

Learning aids: Some variety in materials.

Unit interaction: Medium. Often there is the assumption that discussion can be guided for your purposes.

Evaluation: Medium to Low.

Suggestions: Medium. Several sets do offer supplementary aids and ideas.

Integration

Purposes: Like the transmission approach, instills certain values in students. However, this approach underscores *personal* values. Constant themes are the uniqueness of the individual, personal satisfaction in work and leisure, and happy relations with family and peers.

Teacher model: The first role of the teacher is as an accepter. The teacher is to communicate to students the feeling that they are worthwhile, yet noting that all have limitations as well as assets. In addition to playing the role of accepter, the teacher is seen as an enabler, constructing group dynamics and situations which will raise certain personal and social issues for discussions.

Methods: A favorite method would be circle activities and the teacher's use of modeling and positive reinforcement. Games and simulations as well as value sheets would be appropriate for this approach.

Sample activities: Puppet sets which have characters who solve problems are often used in elementary schools. Activities such as a values auction, goal setting, or sharing of feelings are all typical at the secondary level.

Resources: For the teacher's background, several books are recommended.

Gerald Weinstein and Mario Fantini, *Toward Humanistic Education: A Curriculum of Affect* (New York: Praeger, 1970).

Chester Cromwell, *et al., Becoming: A Course in Human Relations* (New York: Lippincott, 1975).

G. William Pfeiffer and John E. Jones, *A Handbook of Structural Experiences for Human Relations Training* (La Jolla, Calif.: University Associates, 1969, 1974).

Carl Fischer and Walter Limbacher, *Dimensions of Personality* (Dayton, Ohio: Pflaum, 1969–70, 1972), grades K–6. Extensive use of worksheets, readings, and small group work is done.

Don Dinkmeyer, *Developing Understanding of Self and Others (DUSO)* (Circle Pines, Minn.: American Guidance Service, 1970–73), grades K–1, 2–4. Through puppets and discussions, the themes of seeing individual differences, building trust, showing feelings, and developing emphatizing skills are treated.

Judith L. Anderson, *et. al., Focus on Self Development* (Chicago: Science Research Associates, 1970–72), grades K–6. Key points are self understanding, problem solving, and developing areas of interest. An elaborate set of black-and-white photographs is used to uncover student feelings.

The Kid Concern, *Friends and Me and You* (San Antonio, Tex.: The Learning about Learning Educational Foundation, 1974), grades K–6. A small packet of activities which is to be used informally to build better human relations.

Harold Bessell and Uvaldo Palomares, *Human Development Program* (La Mesa, Calif.: Human Development Training Institute, 1973, 1974), grades K–6. The three main areas of instruction are awareness (knowing thoughts, feelings, and actions), mastery (knowing abilities and how to use them), and social interaction (knowing other people).

Combined Motivation Education System, Inc., *Motivation Advancement Program (MAP)* (Chicago: Encyclopedia Brittanica Corporation, 1971), grades 7–12. Follows certain ideas of William Glasser about the importance of building successful experiences through learning about one's strengths and needs and doing realistic goal setting.

Henry Dupont, *et al.*, *Toward Affective Development* (TAD) (Circle Pines, Minn.: American Guidance Service, 1974), grades 3–6. Using role-playing and brain-storming techniques, TAD stresses exploration of feelings and development of self-concept.

Assessment of integration:

Values concepts: Medium to low. The general terminology used for the variety of personal and social goals produces some confusion within the sets.

Activities: Objectives similarly are of quite a range in clarity.

Learning aids: High. Many types and format, ranging from the theraputic to the petty.

Unit interaction: Medium. Stress is on much interaction and is usually explained well.

Evaluation: Medium. Some attempts at measurement are made, including standardized instruments.

Suggestions: High. Most sets encourage flexibility as conditions warrant.

Values Clarification

Purposes: To help students to become aware of their own values and those of others and to develop skills to communicate their values. Learners are to use both rational thinking and emotional strategies to examine their personal feelings, values, and behavior patterns.

Teacher model: The teacher would be a trainer, primarily, providing students with the skills needed to clarify their values. However, since values must be shared and acted upon, the teacher would also express his or her own point of view.

Methods: Value sheets and clarifying questions are the most frequently used. Typical activities include rank orders, distributions, and questions which ask for short answers. More strategies would be done by the individual than in groups.

Sample activities: Distributions and value-voting games would be chosen often at the elementary level; continuums, diaries, and simulations are used at the secondary level.

Resources: Basic texts for the teacher are:

Louis Raths, Merrill Harmin, and Sidney B. Simon, *Values and Teaching* (Columbus, Ohio: Merrill, 1966, 1977).
Sidney B. Simon, Leland Howe, and Howard Kirschenbaum, *Values Clarification* (New York: Hart, 1972).[10]

Curriculum materials include:

William F. Goodykoonz, *Contact* (New York: Scholastic Book Services, 1968–74), grades 7–12. The thirteen units in this set extensively use reading anthologies. A favorite strategy is to ask students to keep logbooks.

H. B. Gelatt, Barbara Varenhorst, Richard Carey, and Gordon P. Miller, *Deciding* and *Decisions and Outcomes* (Princeton, N.J.: College Entrance Examination Board, 1972, 1973), grades 7–9, 10–12. Emphasis is upon decision-making skills through activities such as games, simulations, and value sheets which raise questions about the risks learners are willing to take to gain career satisfaction and personal happiness.

Peter McPhail, Hilary Chapman, J. R. Ungoed-Thomas, and Lillian Teeman, *Lifelife* (Niles, Ill.: Argus, 1975), grades 7–12. The authors suggest that you do not use this material as the basis of a separate course, but integrate it into subject matter areas. Themes include learning to care and "What would you have done?"

Merrill Harmin, *Making Sense of Our Lives* (Niles, Ill.: Argus, 1974), grades 7–12. A collection of value sheets, cassettes, and discussion strategies which focus on personal growth. Many current issues are covered.

Carl Elder, *Making Value Judgments: Decisions for Today* (Columbus, Ohio: Merrill, 1972), grades 7–12. A one-text curriculum which uses some value clarification and biographical essays to raise questions about the students' decisions on use of drugs, smoking, and career choices.

John G. Church, *A Probe Into Values* (New York: Harcourt, 1973), grades 4–6. A series of pamphlets with values clarification strategies, focusing on use in small groups.

Ronald Klein, *Search for Meaning* (Dayton, Ohio: Pflaum/Standard, 1974), grades 7–8. A large collection of ditto masters which centers on such topics as family, friendship, and pressure.

Gerri Curwin and Richard Curwin, *Search for Values* (Dayton, Ohio: Pflaum/Standard, 1972), grades 9–12. A set of value sheets organized around the themes of competition, time, personal space, etc.

M. F. Smith, *The Valuing Approach to Career Education* (Waco, Tex.: Educational Achievement Corporation, 1973–74), grades K–8. A wide variety of instructional materials and media are used to raise value questions about career development, including leisure. It has been field-tested extensively.

Rodney Allen, *et. al., Values Education Series* (Evanston, Ill.: McDougal, Littell and Company, 1973, 1974), grades 9–12. The three major areas of study are the environment, society, and power. A sample title is "Deciding How to Live on Spaceship Earth." Readings are the primary method of instruction.

Assessment of values clarification:

Value concepts: Medium to low. Most sets are collections of strategies and show little concern for theory.

Activities: Medium. Objectives are informal.

Learning aids: Medium. Heavy concentration on value sheets and discussions.

Unit interaction: High. Instructions are usually explained and student interest is high.

Evaluation: Low. Little concern is expressed for systematic evaluation.

Suggestions: High. There is much encouragement for modification and flexibility.

Action

Purposes: Similar to those listed under analysis and clarification. Urges students to act on their personal and social convictions.

Teacher model: In addition to being a guide suggesting topics for research, the teacher is an investigator, exploring with students problems in the community.

Methods: Superka notes that the two techniques unique to this system are skill practice in group organization and stress on action projects.[11]

Sample activities: Elementary classes would typically write letters to the editors and do comparison shopping, while learners at the high-school level might use case studies and investigative action on credit practices. Both levels might use consumer education kits distributed by such firms as J. C. Penney.

Resources: For the teacher, see Fred M. Newman, *Education for Citizen Action: Challenge for Secondary Curriculum* (Berkeley: McCutchan, 1975).

Curriculum materials include:

Fred M. Newman and Donald W. Oliver, *Social Action: Dilemmas and Strategies* (Columbus, Ohio: Xerox, 1972), grades 9–12. A single resource for teachers, it also is the manual for the Values Education Series previously discussed.

W. Ron Jones, *Finding Community: A Guide to Community Research and Action* (Palo Alto, Calif.: Freel, 1971), grades 9–12. Several activities from this curriculum have already been mentioned (the investigations and letters to editors).

The Citizenship Education Clearing House, P. O. Box 24220, St. Louis, Missouri 63130, offers lists of action projects.

Minnesota State Department of Education, *Environmental Action Cards* (1974), grades 1–6.[12] While this set uses clarifying questions frequently, it also provides a significant number of action strategies. Rather than being centered on changing community wrongs, they relate to such topics as global awareness. Uses such techniques as trying out new foods and dances.

J. A. Swan and W. B. Stapp (eds.), *Environmental Education: Strategies Toward a More Livable Future* (Beverly Hills, Calif.: Sage Publications, Halsted Press 1974), grades 7–12.[13]

National Commission on Resources for Youth, *New Roles for Youth in the School and Community* (Englewood Cliffs, N.J.: Citation Press, 1974), grades 10–12. Included are descriptions of seventy action and service projects.

Assessment of action:

Values concepts: Medium.
Activities: High.
Learning Aids: Medium to low. Rather than external media, the stress is on first-hand experience.

Unit interaction: High. Usually well explained.

Evaluation: Low to medium. Teacher and students will have to see results.

Suggestions: Medium to high. There is an awareness that improvisation is necessary.

Evocation

Purposes: To increase students' ability to more openly and freely express their spontaneous reactions to aesthetic stimuli and heighten their sensitivities to tastes, sounds, smells, and textures. Further, this approach encourages learners to share their emotions more openly because it believes that many decisions are made on emotional grounds. Basically it is a "reactionary" position which believes that too much attention has been paid to cognitive goals in school.

Teacher model: The teacher is a stimulator who provides resources which are heavily laden with value messages and which require students to react sensually.

Methods: Highly structured lesson plans are ruled out by some advocates of this approach. There is a strong reliance on posters, photographs, objects, and readings which evoke strong reactions.

Sample activities: At the elementary level class members are blindfolded and concentrate upon the textures and smells of various objects. A series of war pictures might be used to ferret out secondary students' feelings about war and peace.

Resources:

Bob Eberle and Rosie Emery Hall, *Affective Education Guidebook: Classroom Activities in the Realm of Feelings* (Buffalo: D.O.K. Publishers, 1975).

Robert E. Samples, "Value Prejudice: Toward a Personal Awareness," *Media and Methods* (September 1974), pp. 14–18, 49–52. A salient statement on evocation.

Harry S. Broudy, *Enlightened Cherishing: An Essay on Aesthetic Education* (Urbana: University of Illinois Press, 1972). A more thorough philosophical review.

Alice K. Gordon, *Games for Growth* (Boston: Beacon, 1972). A textbook which provides a number of suggestions consistent with this approach.

Gloria A. Castillo, *Left-Handed Teaching* (New York: Praeger, 1974). A somewhat similar text, but one which focuses more on touching activities.

There are not many curriculum sets in this field, partly due to the strong feelings of some advocates that affective learning should not be highly structured. Several of the resources cited here are related to literature. For example, Random House (New York) produced the *Creative Writing Bug* series in 1968 for grades 4–6. More recently, the National Council of Teachers of English (Urbana, Illinois) has published resource books for teachers such as David Bleick, *Readings and Feelings* (1975).

Self-Expression and Conduct: The Humanities (New York: Harcourt, 1974–75), grades 1–3. Has many elements that would relate to the evocation approach.

Creating Characterization (New York: Viking Press, 1973), grades 5–8. Good materials whose major purpose is to create aesthetic sensitivity.

Essence I and *Essence II* (Reading, Mass.: Addison-Wesley, 1971, 1975), grades 7–12. Also create aesthetic sensitivity.

Photograph sets and poster sets from Argus, Augsburg Press, and MAP, to be discussed in chapter 4, would also be useful.

Assessment of evocation:

Value concepts: Low. Most sets have little structure.
Activities: High. Objectives are simply stated.
Learning aids: Medium to low. Highly subjective.
Unit interaction: Medium. Hard to predict outcome.
Evaluation: Teacher must evaluate the depth of feelings expressed in the group.
Suggestions: Varies considerably with sets.

Union

Purposes: To aid students in reflecting upon the unity of the world (cosmos) and to build the student's sense of inner contentment. This may or may not be associated with theological positions. This approach would encompass those who hold that the individual is a lost and sinful being who must give himself up to a divine will, as well as those who believe meditation which places one in harmony with the universe is sufficient.

Teacher role: The teacher is chiefly a harmonizer, which includes being both a model of acceptable behavior and a resource for the methods and materials which could be used to attain union.

Methods: There are a wide variety of teaching techniques for this approach, including transcendental meditation, prayer, self-hypnosis, dream analysis, reference to conversion experiences, and readings of philosophers and theologians.

Resources: This is an expanding area which offers little in the way of formal curriculum sets.[14] Introductory materials would include:

George Brown, *Human Teaching for Human Learning* (New York: Viking, 1971).

Abraham Maslow (ed.), *New Knowledge in Human Values* (New York: Harper, 1959), especially D. T. Suzuki, "Human Values in Zen," pp. 94–106.[15]

Assessment of union:

Values concepts: Difficult to assess, due to variety.
Activities: Low. For many, the objectives are loosely stated.
Learning aids: Extreme variety.
Unit interaction: Again, hard to categorize, because unity through individual contemplation is stressed.
Evaluation: Low. If anything, it is based on testimonials.
Suggestions: Hard to assess, considering the diverse forms this approach takes.

Investment

Purposes: To help individuals analyze and change their value positions through a systematic blend of cognitive and affective activities requiring investments of time, effort, and finances.

Teacher model: The teacher is like an investment counselor or broker, exposing students to various options they have for risking their talents and goals. Also, he or she serves as an evaluator, helping students see the payoff on their choices.

Methods: The favorite activity is construction or model building, which asks participants to build a symbol of their point of view. A number of strategies are borrowed from the other approaches, typically those which take time to do and which often suggest an action as the natural conclusion of the activity.

Sample activities: At the elementary level culture kits could be constructed, and distribution games played. For secondary students, such activities as designing a bumper sticker or producing a personality box would be typical. See chapter 7 for numerous activities.

Resources: Chapter 1 described in part the philosophical basis of this approach. It takes a wholistic view of man as advocated by such writers as Philip Phenix and Martin Buber.[16]

I have developed a V-A-L-U-E-S format, which is somewhat similar to the systematic approach adopted by the *Skills for Ethical Action* course prepared by Research for Better Schools.[17]

Assessment of values investment:

Values concepts: Medium to high. Major point is that some value positions are to be affirmed.

Activities: High. Clear understanding of what is expected to result from activity.

Learning Aids: High. Use of many resources.

Unit interaction: Medium to high. There should be a high degree of learner involvement.

Evaluation: Medium. An area which calls for more research and field-testing.

Suggestions: High. Should be very flexible.

Notes

1. Douglas Superka, *et. al., Values Education Sourcebook* (Boulder, Col.: Social Science Education Consortium, 1976). In chapter 2 an earlier document by Superka was referred to. This is an update. If you wish a more detailed look at the typologies, consult Douglas P. Superka, "A Typology of Valuing Theories and Values Education Approaches" (Unpublished doctoral dissertation, University of California, 1973).

2. Marjorie E. Kelly, *In Pursuit of Values* (New York: Paulist Press, 1973). Also see Howard A. Ozmon and Joseph Johnson, "Value Implications in Children's Reading Material," *The Reading Teacher* **22**, no. 3 (December 1968): 246–301. John R. Meyer (ed.), *Reflections on Values Education* (Waterloo, Ont.: Wilfrid Laurier University, 1976). John Miller, *Humanizing in the Classroom: Models of Teaching in Affective Education* (New York: Praeger, 1976).

3. Morton Alpern, "Curriculum Significance of the Affective Domain," *Theory into Practice* **13**, no. 1 (February 1974): 46–53. Andrew Rembert, "Teaching about Values: Remaining Neutral vs. Advocating One's Own View," *Peabody Journal of Education* **53**, no. 2 (January 1976): 71–75. Also see Cleo Cherryholmes, "Toward a Theory of Social Education," (Department of Health, Education and Welfare, 1971), ED 065 373.

4. Rodney Allen, "Teaching about Religion," *Religion in Elementary Social Studies Teacher Self-Instructional Kit II* (Tallahassee: Religion-Social Studies Curriculum Project, Florida State University, 1973), pp. 8–11.

5. Richard L. Curwin and Barbara S. Fuhrmann, *Discovering Your Teaching Self: Humanistic Approaches to Effective Teaching* (Englewood Cliffs, N.J.: Prentice-Hall, 1975).

6. Superka, *Values Education Sourcebook*, pp. 3–6.

7. For a review of the controversy and decisions by the United States Supreme Court on teaching about religion in the public schools, see the American Association of School Administrators, *Religion in the Public Schools* (New York: Harper Chapelbooks, 1964). For a synopsis of Phenix's position and more recent discussion on the topic, see *Religious Education* **71**, no. 1 (January–February 1976): 68–95.

8. A. J. Grainger, *The Bullring* (Oxford: Pergamon Press, 1970), p. 5.

9. I am reminded of Jonathan Kozol's decision in *Death at an Early Age* (New York: Houghton Mifflin, 1967), when he drops the formal curriculum and chooses material more relevant to the students in the Boston ghetto school. The constant dilemma we all face is like the one faced by the Puritans: How long can we stay and fight to improve life before we decide that to stay will end in our becoming tainted and ultimately corrupted? See also James P. Shaver, "Considerations Underlying a Public Issue Oriented Social Studies Curriculum" (Department of Health, Education and Welfare, 1964), ED 065 386.

10. Howard Glaser-Kirschenbaum and Barbara Glaser-Kirschenbaum, "An An-

notated Bibliography on Values Clarification," in Simon and Kirschenbaum (eds.), *Readings*, pp. 368–85.

11. Superka, *Values Education Sourcebook*, p. 178.

12. The address of the Minnesota State Department of Education is 642 Capitol Square Building, St. Paul, Minnesota 55101.

13. Also Clifford E. Knapp, "Teaching Environmental Education with a Focus on Values" (Department of Health, Education and Welfare, 1972), ED 070 614.

14. Superka, *Values Education Sourcebook*, pp. 193–95.

15. For a discussion of transcendental meditation and schooling, see Francis Driscoll, "TM as a Secondary School Subject," *Kappan* **54**, no. 4 (December 1972): 236–37.

16. Philip Phenix, *Realms of Meaning* (New York: McGraw-Hill, 1964); Martin Buber, *Between Man and Man* (New York: Macmillan, 1965).

17. Marian L. Chapman, "Skills for Ethical Action Instructional Materials, An Overview," *Research for Better Schools, Inc.* (July 1975) (in-house publication). Also see note 13, chapter 2, above.

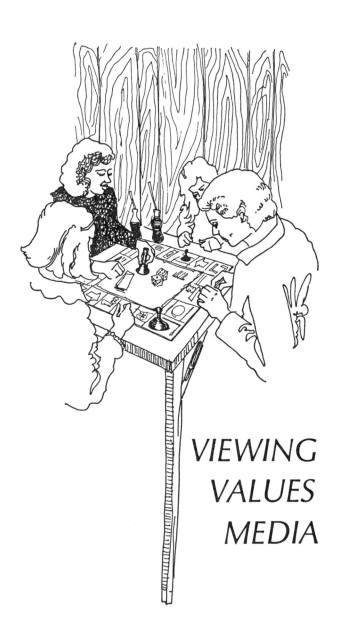

VIEWING
VALUES
MEDIA

As an educator you have many choices to make about the media you will use. Chapter 3 discussed formal curriculum sets. Chapter 4 focuses on media available as instructional tools for values education. Because any long list of media would soon be obsolete, this chapter emphasizes the agencies which you can contact for media. Further, the chapter stresses the strengths and weaknesses of various media.

The major topics covered in chapter 4 include an overview of media's advantages, a survey of techniques and suggestions for "local" media, and a list of general reference works and agencies. The largest section lists media by category (television series and videotapes; poster and photograph sets; simulations; records and cassettes; and films, filmloops, filmstrips, and slides) and describes the advantages and disadvantages of each.

Within professional organizations, such as the American Association of School Librarians and the Association for Educational Communication and Technology, the term *media* refers to "all modes of communication, including print and audiovisual forms, and their accompanying technology."[1] Arbitrarily, my definition is less encompassing. Chapter 3 dealt with curriculum sets, some of which include some audiovisual materials. Chapter 4 focuses on those nonprint educational materials which will most likely be used as supplementary resources rather than as a basic text or resource.

WHAT MEDIA
CAN DO

In America today we are bombarded by a wide variety of commercial media. While television, radio, the movies, and the newspapers are the most obvious, we are subject also to the stimuli of blinking neon advertisements, boldly colored brochures and letterheads in our mail, and the mobile murals on passing trucks and railroad cars. Considering the impact of television only, it is no wonder that media has been called "the third parent." According to several studies, children entering kindergarten have already watched 4,000 hours of television; and by the time they are high school seniors they will have logged approximately 15,000 hours, 3,000 hours more than they will have spent in school. And although it may seem that television has eclipsed radio, statistics indicate that Americans still listen to more than three hours of radio every day.

Such data are important to you as an educator. As you plan your classroom activities, you have to be increasingly aware of the experiences students have gained through media. You should ask yourself: Are my presentations one dimensional, that is, consistently the same format? Will the use of media help? If so, what instructional technology should I use?

Potency of Media

According to its advocates, media offers a number of advantages which can markedly improve the learning environment.

Both common sense and research tell us that learning improves when we *change the pace.* Typically, using media increases the senses learners use. The variety helps build attention span and increases interest level.

Effective use of media *heightens concentration.* The darkened room, the vivid colors on the screen, the movement, and the musical background help the students focus upon the material's concepts.

Media can *condense time and space.* Think of a time-lapse film which shows the movement of clouds or the growth of a plant, and how much more graphic they are than teachers describing the same processes. Or, although a students may have some conception of the distance between two countries, a well-illustrated map can make the distance more comprehensible.

One basic purpose of all instruction is to *transmit knowledge.* Toward that end, media can clear up misconceptions. Have you ever formed a mental image of a desert, or of an ethnic group, or an animal, based on a verbal description, only to have it radically altered by a still photograph which showed that your imagination and your prejudices had been wrong.

Media can also *create a climate* which enhances or retards learning. The foreign language instructor playing music from the native country may build an atmosphere which encourages students to enter into the "spirit" of the other nation. Aesthetic awareness can open learners to ideas and facts they had not contemplated.

Through demonstration, media can *teach skills.* A videotape of a sports routine can give a novice insight on what is needed for mastery. The recording of your voice repetitively can alert you to errors in speech patterns, which you can then correct.

Teachers can use media to *show relationships.* Charts and graphs can dramatically portray comparisons. A class-built miniature landscape, complete with "river," can be used to show the causes and effects of erosion.

Certain types of media are especially good for *reframing reality.* What is small can be enlarged; what is fast can be slowed down; what is complex can be simplified.

Such media as educational games, role playing, and 16 mm film can come close to *simulating reality.* Unlike some other educational strategies, including tests and questionnaires, which do not encourage involvement, certain forms of media commit students to interaction and decision making.

Finally, when powerfully done, media can *move individuals to action.* Films on injustice have prompted some people to reexamine their own beliefs and change behavior. Think of the radio play "The War of the Worlds," which threw many people into a panic.[2]

Media Theory

While we may acknowledge the many fine characteristics of media, we often ignore them. We may choose a film or record because it's available at the moment or because it's inexpensive. To review the effectiveness and efficiency of various media, let's look at several texts.[3]

Edgar Dale's *Audio-Visual Methods in Teaching* is perhaps best known. Dale's "cone of experience" (see Figure 4–1) rates media in terms of degrees of realism. Dale cautions educators not to think of the higher levels of abstraction as "good" or "bad." The subject matter and the ages of learners determine what is appropriate. Nevertheless, Dale is criticized for favoring realism too much; some critics argue that too much realism can be distracting.

Using Dale's model, Leslie Briggs argues that the levels are somewhat related to the age of the learner. Since the higher levels are more abstract and make it easier to compress learning time, teachers should go as low as necessary to insure success and as high as possible for efficiency. Teachers should select low layers for "slow but sure" learning, higher layers for "potentially fast but risky" learning.[4]

Walter Wager posits that Dale's cone should be used to weigh affective changes. He believes that the media at the top of the cone will probably be most efficient in establishing attitudes in adults or changing the attitudes of young people. To change attitudes of adults or establish attitudes in younger people, the lower levels of the cone will probably be most effective. (For Wager, effectiveness is described as the extent to which the desired objective is reached; efficiency refers to the "cost" of being effective in terms of time and/or resources).[5]

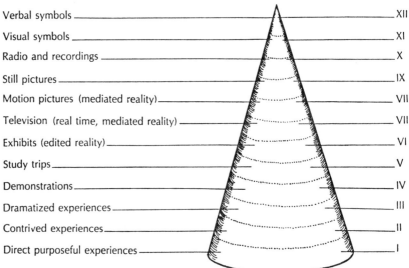

Levels of Abstraction

Verbal symbols ——— XII
Visual symbols ——— XI
Radio and recordings ——— X
Still pictures ——— IX
Motion pictures (mediated reality) ——— VIII
Television (real time, mediated reality) ——— VII
Exhibits (edited reality) ——— VI
Study trips ——— V
Demonstrations ——— IV
Dramatized experiences ——— III
Contrived experiences ——— II
Direct purposeful experiences ——— I

Figure 4–1   *Dale's Cone of Experience.*   From AUDIO-VISUAL METHODS IN TEACHING, THIRD EDITION, by Edgar Dale. Copyright © 1946, 1954, 1969, by Holt, Rinehart and Winston, Inc. Reprinted by permission of Holt, Rinehart and Winston.

Since this is not a media textbook, I would prefer to direct you to texts which detail the advantages and disadvantages of various media. One source is Haney and Ullmer's *Educational Communications and Technology.*[6] Interestingly, few methodology-of-media texts incorporate research which verifies the techniques described. I am hard-pressed to tell you that films can or cannot accomplish such-and-such or that cassettes, for certain, can bring about such-and-such a change.

If there is a consistent point made in the media textbooks, it seems to be the rule that the higher degree of student involvement, the greater chance of effective learning. This seems to disagree somewhat with Dale's position on the "goodness" or "badness" of media.[7]

We have been talking about realism and levels of abstraction related to learning generally and to student involvement in particular. The following activity demands a high degree of involvement and usually produces a spirited discussion.

Value Activity: "Life Strip"

On the "life strip" illustrate nine significant events in your life through symbols. Share it with a friend and discuss how similar or dissimilar your events are. Is much of your life centered around one institution —family, church, school? Were these events controversial? In the first six boxes draw symbols which show significant events in your life. In the last three boxes, indicate what major events you would like to have happen to you in the future.

FUTURE	FUTURE	FUTURE

Value identification: "Life Strip."

Activity: Students will create a panel of graphic symbols which reveal significant events of their lives, that is, a "life strip."

Learning aids: A handout with nine squares. Color ballpoints or crayons are helpful.

Unit interaction: Senior high–Adult. Very few instructions are needed. If it is to be done in class, allow at least forty-five minutes for the activity. The questions for discussion may be withheld. Appoint a member of each subgroup you form to be the reporter at the end of the session.

Evaluation: See discussion questions above. Additional questions: Are the events you selected spread out over a number of years or clustered? Are the events you selected typically positive or negative?

Suggestions: This is easy to convert to other formats. To encourage more of an artistic effort, each student could develop a flip chart or possibly a filmstrip. Circumstances may suggest that this not be a shared activity, but an inclusion in a diary.

"DO IT YOURSELF" MEDIA

You may be assuming after reading this far that *media* most often refers to commercially produced products you will have to rent or purchase. While the chapter does discuss what you may gain from regional or national outlets, you can *easily* produce or locate media to use with your students.

I am deeply indebted to a former professor, Oscar Rumpf, who once enumerated "thirty-two ways to tell a story."[8] I would like to modify some of his suggested methods, but retain his central idea: A teacher can find many creative methods to approach any educational assignment.

In the Classroom

It is probably safe to assume that during your teaching career, regardless of the grade level or subject matter, you will be asked to relate some details about the life of a famous person to your students. Let's assume too you're asked to do more than simply pass on facts. You're to relay some of the "contributions" this person made, or to describe his or her values. In what ways could you approach the assignment, building student interest without "moralizing"?

1. Through lecture or assigned readings about the person, we expect students to build interest. But if it is important to interest students in an individual, a livelier way to do it is to direct them to *primary documents.* Have them read the diaries the person wrote, or letters written by friends and enemies. If you are studying local heroes and heroines, have students visit the county courthouse to find copies of their wills or descriptions of their property. If they did extensive writings, it is relatively easy to find reference books which comment on drafts of their famous speeches or essays.

2. Students are often interested in family dynamics. Construct *diagrams* of family trees. Did the person come from a famous family? Was he or she first-born or the youngest?

3. A *time line* can establish for the student some comparisons with other periods. What was going on in the world just before and just after this person lived? Was he ahead of his time?

4. Because we so often place famous people on pedestals, they lose their humaneness. It can be helpful to build a *chart or graph* to show the "crises" the person experienced. Students might then relate similar experiences.

For example:

Age 6	Age 13	Age 18	Age 24	
				what she did
				what I was doing

5. Often we study isolated events in or comments about an individual's life, and do not recognize the mosaic of his world or the richness which it might have had. A group *frieze or mural* which details the many facets of the person and his era can be very meaningful.

6. What was the world (or nation or county) like when this person lived? Were they on the frontier? Part of a minority surrounded by hostile groups? What type of climate was prevalent? A *map or globe* might be the key to students raising new questions.

7. The much-maligned *bulletin board* could come to the rescue. Reserve a portion of it for student reports about the person under study. If it is a local figure, perhaps a page from the paper could be photocopied and placed on the board. If it is a current figure, the students could organize a "clipping service."

8. Although commercial posters are available, it is easy to construct homemade *posters,* which might illustrate a famous quotation from the individual. Or an outline of the person's head and the colors used to decorate the poster could begin a discussion about the feelings students have about him.

9. *Chalkboards,* and to a lesser extent *flip charts,* are so obvious they are often overlooked for use with historical study. Over a period of time students could develop a list of characteristics of the individual. Honest academic scholarship would require that such lists show "warts and all."

10. The popularity of cartoon strips is not just a modern phenomenon. Resource books will contain *cartoons* and *sketches* of famous people, or at least of their period. How were they treated by friends and enemies?

11. A traditional approach to education is to have the school library or instructional materials center (IMC) stock reproductions of *famous paintings* of notable people. Even if that's all that's available, it can be interesting to accumulate a series of pictures showing the maturing of the person. If the school does not have many pictures, a class project might be locating high-quality illustrations to build up the school collection.

12. The *kamishabi* originated in Japan. It is a series of uniform-size flat pictures placed together and held in a vertical position on a table or stand. The storyteller interprets the front picture by reading off the back of the last picture. The procedure is to remove the first picture from the front to the rear. The back of the first picture contains the story of the second picture. This could be an excellent class project—to design a kamishabi which could be presented to another class.

13. Your students may be interested in building a mini-TV or *picturol,* sometime. It is a series of pictures glued or drawn on a roll of paper. The ends of the roll are attached to dowels or pieces of broomsticks inserted in a box. The box front is cut to look like a television screen, and the documentary is shown.

Figure 4–2.

14. Certain occasions may allow you to display objects owned by the character you're studying. An *opaque projector* permits every member of a large class to view, simultaneously, both small drawings and objects.

15. Perhaps you are studying an artist. If there are enough pictures of the artist's work, or you can actually photograph sculptures, consider making a *slide* set. Illustrations from magazines may be photographed with the aid of a copy stand, and you can even lift the picture from certain periodicals.[9] If you know of certain pictures you want, but you do not have them immediately available, try writing government and commercial agencies.[10]

16. Carrying the slide concept one step further, it is possible to construct a *filmstrip* at a nominal charge. Check with your local camera shops. Or you may wish to buy blank filmstrips on which the class can try to imitate the style of the artist you are studying.[11]

17. To dramatize some biographical studies, *symbols* could be used. Show the family crest or the emblem of the political party in power at that time.

18. A *diorama,* or three-dimensional picture viewed through an opening, could portray scenes from the person's early life. A common container for a diorama is a shoe box. In it, to scale, you could build the interior of the person's home, or depict an event which brought him or her national fame.

19. If you are focusing on a person from another culture you may find *display boards* a helpful aid. Flannelgraph boards are especially good with younger children because they are easy to work with and the bright colors attract the children. Use outing flannel for background strips, and paste small pieces of flannel on the backs of the illustrations to be used to tell the story. Hook and loop boards have become popular, especially because of their ability to hold large and heavy items. Again, small pieces of the hook and loop might be attached to such artifacts as coins, tools, musical instruments, and weapons.

20. If your students have a dramatic flair, you might try a *tableau* or "still" living picture. Recreate a famous painting, or act out a crisis event. On a smaller scale, you might ask learners to choose their favorite characters and have them come dressed as those people. Take pictures of the class.

21. *Puppets and marionettes* are powerful attention-getters, as *Sesame Street* has demonstrated. Bodies for hand puppets can be made from cloth remnants and their heads from such materials as boxes, bags, wood, stuffed socks, and balls. Marionettes require more skill to construct and manipulate than puppets, but they make it possible to use

more elaborate design. If you are pressed for time, use old dolls for the marionettes.[12]

22.   Today you and your students probably have easy access to cameras. Arrange to take *photographs* of interesting local citizens. Or visit a local newspaper and go through their picture files. If you are able to look at pictures of individuals over a period of years, what conclusions do you come to about their lifestyles?

23.   Don't forget the feelings of immediacy generated by *recordings and tapes.* Public libraries and school IMC's often have collections of famous speeches and music from different periods and cultures which could help you develop a "you are there" or "time capsule" radio or television program.

24.   *Film loops and films (8 mm)* will be more expensive than most other aids suggested, but can be worth the cost, time, and effort required to make them. Remember that each film loop should convey a single concept. In three minutes could your class portray the concept of civil disobedience advocated by Martin Luther King? Using cartoon drawings, could the class script and produce a short 8 mm film on the efforts to gain equal voting rights for women?[13]

25.   A favorite hobby of elementary school children is *model building.* It is fairly easy to locate commercially made models which students have built that could be used to spark discussions on such general topics as prehistoric culture, wars, violence in society, and space exploration. It is possible now to get models of famous buildings, in keeping with literary and historical themes.[14]

Community Resources

These suggestions show that certain readily available materials can magnify your value discussions. And there are many other resources and techniques to which you can turn, as well.

1.   *Field trips.* Depending on the size of your community, you may have a number of places which students would like to visit, individually or as a class. In almost every town there are a variety of retail stores, businesses, and service agencies whose personnel would be willing to describe their occupations to students. You can visit museums, hospitals, fire and police stations, as well as social clubs, company offices, and factories.

2.   *Speakers.* You may find that time will not permit you to make as many trips as you wish. Perhaps you could survey the class to find out what kinds of careers they are interested in and invite representatives of those occupations to speak in your classroom.

3.   *Craftsmen and hobbyists.* Check with your local newspaper to find out what kind of special interest clubs there are in your community.

Demonstrations of special skills and unique collections can both reveal the values of some local citizens and spark the interests of a lethargic class. Imagine discussing the American frontier from the different perspectives of an Indian artist whose works depict the tribe's communion with nature and a model railroader who displays the iron horses which radically altered the western plains.

4. *Representatives of ethnic groups.* It is a rare town which does not have at least two or three ethnic groups of some size. You can probably find social clubs or individuals willing to show off the customs, music, costumes, favorite foods, and values of their ancestors.[15]

5. *Research projects.* Someone in your class may develop an interest in a special value topic. What did the founders of your city cherish? Perhaps he might visit the local cemetery and do a tombstone rubbing.[16] Another student may be nudged by a television documentary to explore attitudes toward prison reform. You could guide her in the interviewing of court and penal officials, the prisoners, and people on the street. Several students might decide to find out what types of transportation are most often used in their neighborhoods and report their findings through a photo essay.

The list could go on and on, but enough ideas have been given to reinforce my major point. Don't neglect the numerous resources you have in your classroom and in the community which can enhance your discussions of value topics.

Value Activity: "Do You Get the Picture?"

The goal of this activity is to make a film which conveys to the viewer either a feeling you currently have or a commentary you wish to make about some societal issue. Follow the instructions below on locating film and preparing your film. Then show the film to others and discuss with them how clearly you communicated your value.

Value identification: "Do You Get the Picture?"

Activity: Participant produces a film in which viewers see the maker's personality expressed through a value or a feeling.

Learning aids: **1.**   Either 8 mm or 16 mm film. The latter is easier to work with for this activity, but more expensive. I would recommend, if you are a beginner, that you try 16 mm clear leader film with double sprockets. With that film either side is proper, and it can be marked with a variety of color pens. It can be purchased through photo supply stores or university media centers.

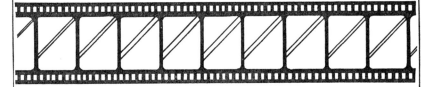

Figure 4–3.   *Double Sprocket Film*

Black leader 16 mm film will give you more striking color patterns as the vivid hues contrast with the black background, but it does require more work.

One possible source of film may be the local television stations. From time to time stations wish to dispose of old commercials, many of which are on 16 mm film. You should be able to get such films free. Or your school's athletic teams may have game films which are now out of date. Consult film booklets on the process of soaking old film in a bleach solution overnight to get a semiclear leader film the next day!

If you are forced to buy film, you may have to use 8 mm film instead of the 16 mm because of cost.

2.   Editing supplies. Locate a film splicer, either splicing tape or glue, and (optional) sharp instruments such as razor blades or hobby knives to scratch the emulsion side of black film.

3.   Coloring supplies. Locate marking pens, grease pencils, etc., which will work with the type of film you have. Typically, ballpoint or felt pens will not work on film.

4. Projection equipment. Find a projector which is correct for the type of film you have. You may wish to enhance the visual message with a cassette musical recording.

Unit interaction: After you have gathered all the supplies together, think through which type of film you are going to make, a "feeling" film or a "persuasion" film. Remember that a 16 mm film is divided into frames, or individual still pictures. At normal speed, a 16 mm film will use up 24 frames per second! You will have to use a lot of frames to convey an idea. For example, let's say you want to demonstrate an explosion of joy you've been feeling. You could start with a tiny ball of red or yellow which grows ever so slowly and finally bursts. Your dots might be this size. . . . . . for sixty frames or more, then this size over the next sixty to eighty ● ● ● ● ● ● ● ● ● ● ● ● ● ● ● , and on to this size ● ● ● ● ● ● ● ● ● ● ● ● ● ● , and finally ● ● ● ● ● ● ● ● ● ● .

Films which express emotion can be done with lots of color and very little drawing. Wavy lines, bold swirls, darting arrows, alternating squares, or circles of solid color can blend into a striking moving portrait!

If you wish to use the black film leader, you have to remove the emulsion and fill the scratched areas with color. The emulsion side is the dull side of the film. If you have decided to make a message film, you do not need to bleach out the old television commercials on them. Splice various bits of commercials together so that they produce a conclusion you would like to see. Or possibly you want to say something which could be expressed simply through several key words or symbols. For example, if you are concerned most about the world's need for peace, you might show the word "peace" being slowly assembled from blocks, and slowly crumbling.

Evaluation: A discussion following the viewing of the film. It is essential to see if others did get the message you wished to convey.

Suggestions: If time permits, make an animated film as a group project. The simplest format is to place some kraft paper on the floor and color a plain background. Make oaktag figures with joints held together by paper brads. You will need a camera which allows you to shoot a few frames before changing the shape of the characters.

Another alternative is to arrange for a film showing which portrays a moral dilemma. You should stop the film, if you need to, before the dilemma is solved. Have students script and film or video tape their solution.

RESOURCES AND
SAMPLE PROGRAMS

Here is a list of materials which will be helpful to the practicing educator. They have been chosen for ease in obtaining them and cost. Because there are numerous books which more specifically list resources under the categories detailed below, I have not given more than a few examples of each resource. To make the list of resources as helpful as possible, a code of age-level is occasionally used (P = nursery through primary; I = intermediate; J = junior high; S = senior high; A = adult).

General Books and ERIC Citations

The single most helpful sourcebook is Jeffrey Shrank's *Media in Values Education* (Niles, Ill.: Argus, 1970), which contains sections on films, simulations, records, and games. Schrank writes sparkling commentaries which may offend some people's opinions. A number of his references are to religious films. Schrank also wrote *Teaching Human Beings: 101 Subversive Activities for the Classroom* (Boston: Beacon, 1973), which offers a lively collection of strategies for sensory awareness and other affective learning.

A partial listing of media sets and a schema for evaluating them is offered in Douglas Superka, *et al.*, *Values Education Sourcebook* (Boulder, Colo.: Social Science Education Consortium, 1976). Another general reference book is by Farnum Gray and George C. Mager, *Liberating Education* (Berkeley, Calif.: McCutchan, 1973).

For general articles, read Donald R. Greer, "Instructional Media for Teaching About Values," *Social Education* **35**, no. 8 (December 1971): 911–15. Also see John T. Canfield and Mark Phillips, "Humanisticography," *Media and Methods* **8**, no. 1 (September 1971): pp. 41–56.

If you have access to a large college or university library you can no doubt use the ERIC system. ERIC is a collection of sources such as funded research grant reports, conference papers, and government documents which do not usually appear in journals. The monthly ERIC index, *Resources in Education,* abstracts the findings. Some libraries have the documents on microfiche cards. If you wish a copy of any specific document, you can write to the ERIC Document Reproduction Service, P. O. Box 190, Arlington, Virginia 22210. Always refer to the number given to each entry when ordering.

References to values education materials include R. C. Hawley and I. L. Hawley, *Handbook of Personal Growth Activities for Classroom Use,* (Amherst, Mass.: Education Research Associates, 1972); Department of Health, Education and Welfare, ED 080 425, a resource listing for elementary grades, and ED 097 269, *Moral and Values Education. Bibliographies in Education, No. 44.*

Ordering Services and Catalogs of Free Materials

Several organizations provide catalogs which give lengthy descriptions of media related to values education, human relations, citizenship, and moral education.

Educators Progress Service, Inc., Randolph, Wisconsin, 53956. Mary Foley Horkheimer and John C. Diffor are editors of such catalogs as "Educator's Guide to Free Filmstrips," "Educator's Guide to Free Films," "Educator's Guide to Free Health, Physical Education, Recreation Materials," and "Educator's Guide to Free Social Studies Materials." Patricia H. Suttles and Raymond Suttles are editors of the "Educator's Grade Guide to Free Teaching Aids," which has special sections on environmental education and global awareness.

Another series of reference works containing values education media is prepared by **NICEM,** the National Information Center for Educational Media. Write the University of Southern California, University Park, Los Angeles, California 90007, for such titles as *Index to Educational Videotapes* and *Index to Educational Records.* Other volumes are available which concentrate upon filmstrips and films and on special topics such as ecology.

If you are interested in multicultural education, see Daniel Sprecher, "Guide to Free-Loan Films about Foreign Lands" (Serina, 1975). Sprecher is also the editor of *Guide to Films (16 mm) About Famous People,* a 1969 volume which contains synopses of over 1,450 motion picture films dealing with over 1,180 individuals, and the *Guide to Films (16 mm) About Negroes* (1970).

Two other helpful reference books are "Audio-Text Cassette Reference Catalog, from The Center for Cassette Studies; and the *Audio-Visual Market Place, A Multimedia Guide 74–75,* R. R. Bowker Company, which contains a list of film distributors.

Government Agencies

If you need to use inexpensive media (and who doesn't these days?), you should consider writing to government agencies. Start, of course, with the Superintendent of Documents, Washington, D.C. 20402, by asking for publications related to your field. For a general reference, see note 11, this chapter.

If you need information about famous individuals and famous events, consider writing the **Library of Congress,** Reference Department or Prints and Photographs Department, Washington, D.C. 20540. You will have to pay for copies of pictures you may want. Allow a substantial period of time for service.

The **U. S. Capitol Historical Society,** 200 Maryland Avenue, N.E., Washington, D.C. 20515, has publications related to the development of the Capitol Building and the early years of the Republic. They also have slides of the more famous paintings in the Capitol.

If you are interested in making slides or prints of famous space scenes, write **NASA** (National Aeronautics and Space Administration), A–V Branch (Code FP), Washington, D.C. 20546. Under certain conditions they will loan you the negatives from which you can make your copies.

The **National Archives,** General Services Administration, Washington, D.C. 20408, can provide you with special collections of art work or photographic reprints on such topics as American Indians, the development of the West, and the role of women in the United States.

If you teach about the role of the military in our nation's past or present, you should consider contacting the various armed forces agencies which maintain extensive film and slide libraries. Through your congressional representative, you can obtain the addresses at the **Pentagon.** One example is the U. S. Army Audio-Visual Agency, the Pentagon, Room 5-A-486, Washington, D.C. 20310.

If your interests run more to the humanities and technological advancements, write such offices as the **National Collection of Fine Arts,** Eighth and G Streets, N.W., Washington, D.C. 20560; the Smithsonian Institution U.S. National Museum, Washington, D. C. 20560; and the **National Endowment for the Humanities,** Washington, D.C. 20506.

The **United States Office of Education,** 400 Maryland Avenue, S.W., Washington, D.C. 20202, has many branches which could help you pursue topics specifically related to education.

One reason for pin-pointing so many places which offer you help is to let you know you do have the budget and the resources to get curricular materials. These agencies, and many others like them, can make your educational task easier and instruction more lively for your class.

Let's turn now to the more traditional types and sources of media, beginning with flat or still pictures.

Posters and Photograph Sets

Ask yourself what photograph is most vivid for you. Is it black-and-white or color? Think of a poster you have seen recently. Why do you think you remembered it?

In historical perspective we can document the importance of still pictures or flat pictures such as photographs and posters. It is believed that a newspaper cartoon about the sinking of the *Lusitania* and then the recruiting poster, "Uncle Sam Wants You," encouraged many people to change their points of view about the first world war. A photograph of Herbert Hoover feeding one of his dogs a steak at the height of the Depression brought out a hostile reaction to him. That still photographs can be as potent as many other forms of art is borne out by the popularity of a museum photography show, "The Family of Man," which later was produced in a book.[17]

Research on the effectiveness of pictures is not conclusive. Some studies suggest that flat pictures can be effective in pointing out prejudices, for example, through individuals revealing their stereotypes about ethnic groups. Other studies suggest that people will share their feelings more easily after viewing pictures than if they were invited to share their feelings without any stimulus.[18]

Instructionally, posters and photographs sets have several advantages. They can be used individually or in sets with a minimum of mechanical effort. You can have the class respond to one picture after an intensive period of focusing on it, or you may leave posters around the room for several days and have students jot down and share their responses informally.

You might consider this approach. First, build a collection of pictures from your own files and invite students to add to it. Make the collection available to the class with the following assignment: Select five to ten which you like. Rank order them, and put them away for a week. Look at them again. Now rank order them again. Has your preference changed? Discard those which you no longer want (place them in the collection again), and pick out several new choices. Continue to do this for several weeks. Then ask yourself what attracted you to the pictures you selected. Do you have a preference for color or black-and-white? Are certain types of scenes dominant, perhaps landscapes, people in fun activities, abstractions, or action shots? Do you prefer stark, simple illustrations or pictures alive with action?

Several disadvantages of still photos should also be mentioned. They include cost, availability, size restrictions, and storage. Another is the difficulty in accurately measuring their impact.

Posters

A number of firms have large collections of posters. One of the most extensive offerings is from Argus Communications. They have sets for various age levels on such topics as being alive, love, ecology, peace, friendship, and soul.

Among the sets by Economic Press is one called *Positive Attitude Posters,* illustrated by Ted Key (who drew the comic strip "Hazel"). It would be appropriate for upper elementary and junior high students. Sample themes are: "Don't fight the inevitable. Cooperate and get it over with," and "The obvious way to GET MORE is to GIVE MORE."

Pennant Educational Materials serves as a clearinghouse for and producer of values education materials. Primary level poster series are on such themes as "Developing my values," "Moods and emotions," and "Understanding my needs." For the intermediate and junior high levels, they offer a set of "posters without words."

Poster sets which have religious themes are available from the Abbey Press.

Several publishing firms which produced curriculum sets described in the preceding chapter also have poster sets. Steck-Vaughn has a set related to their *Human Values* series textbooks. Pflaum/Standard has produced posters in conjunction with their *Dimension of Personality* series. An extensive collection of posters is available from the Motivation Advance Program. They follow the themes of how to make a successful life and how to build better interpersonal relations.

Photograph Sets

The Augsburg Publishing House, 426 S. 5th Street, Minneapolis, Minnesota 55415, has produced a set of photographs entitled "Created Male and Female" which can provoke a spirited discussion about love and sex. It is appropriate for S-A groups.

For subjects such as ecology or conservation, photograph sets are available from such groups as the Sierra Club, 1050 Mills Tower, San Francisco, California 94104. The major oil companies would probably be able to supply you with either photographs or journals which detail their side of the oil crisis. Medical societies such as the American Medical Association and industry groups such as the American Dairy Council provide health charts. You may wish to write journals such as *Learning* magazine (Education Today Company, Inc., 530 University Avenue, Palo Alto, California 94301) for photograph sets and posters. The centerfolds in *Learning* on "law and order" and "appearance" were beamed at the elementary grades.

Certain newspapers, such as the *New York Times,* 229 W. 43rd St., New York, New York 10036, photoduplicate their front pages. Another company, the Pioneer Historical Society, Harriman, Tennessee 37748, reproduces political posters and playbills.

General Materials

If you would like some historical perspective on the use of posters in this country, you can obtain *slides* of representative historical posters through the Sandak Company, 180 Harvard Avenue, Stamford, Connecticut 06902. Consult William Pierson, Jr., and Martha Davidson, *Arts of the United States* (New York: McGraw-Hill, 1960) for illustrations of these posters also.

Another general reference is *Picture Sources* (New York: Special Libraries Association, 1975), which contains hundreds of references for photographs, slides, and other visual materials, mostly free. You may find William Stewart, "A Humanistic Study of the Visual Arts: The Commitment, Risk and Potential," (February, 1972), EJ 051 398, helpful. On the effective use of posters, see Betsy Caprio, *Poster Ideas for Personalized Learning* (Niles, Ill.: Argus, 1975), for the I-A groups.

Records, Tapes, and Multimedia Kits

Flat pictures involve sight, while records and cassettes rely on hearing. Using two senses, seeing and hearing, enhances learning levels appreciably. The problems with using records and cassettes are mechanical ones. You must obtain the equipment and check to make sure it is functioning properly, for example, that the speaker systems are adequate. Another problem is wear and tear on records and tapes, which probably results in heavier replacement rates than for flat pictures.

Records

If you have difficulty locating records through school channels, consult the local library and ask students to bring their favorite albums or singles. An informal record session can be a good way to update everyone on the concerns of youth, the values of leading figures, and issues in the news.

Records can dramatically focus on values issues. For example, at the height of the civil rights movement in the late 1960s, a Broadway play, *In White America,* was recorded.[19] Documentary in style, it claimed to portray the attitudes of whites and blacks toward each other from colonial days to the 1960s. It contained speeches of congressmen and presidents, accounts of the Little Rock school integration effort, and newspaper accounts of trials. The dramatization may be accurate or highly propagandistic, as some critics suggest. But what is important here is that it arouses a strong reaction from listeners. There are other record sets available which attempt to recapture the spirit of various movements through speeches of famous people or music of those times.

While these records may be useful at the secondary level, several record sets offer elementary children unique opportunities. *Dance A Story,* produce by Ginn and Company (1965), is a series of stories which can be acted out creatively. Prentice-Hall has produced *Tunes 'n Tales 'n Things for Children,* which suggests ways primary students can learn about and participate in holidays.

Tapes

As indicated earlier, The Center for Cassette Studies provides a free catalog of cassette tapes on topics such as human violence, the mechanics of moral development, and the future of society. Another agency is Pacifica Tape Library, Department E, 5316 Venice Boulevard, Los Angeles, California 90019. The Human Development Institute, Inc., 43 Old Ivy Road, N.E., Atlanta, Georgia 30305 has a series titled "Encounter Tapes: For Personal Growth." The ten tapes in this adult series, priced at $300, are relatively expensive. Other groups which have tapes available include the National Education Association, Pennant, and Big Sur Recordings.

Multimedia Kits

Several companies have produced kits which they label *multimedia kits.* Some of the most elaborate are from the Encyclopaedia Britannica Educational Corporation (EBEC). *Attitudes* (1973) shows how a young child can cope with discouraging situations. The kit uses six 16 mm films, posters, song cards, and recordings. Another kit for elementary students is called *Creative Expression* (1973). It helps students find new ways to express themselves. Wayne Paulsen is the author of a multimedia kit, *Deciding for Myself* (Winston Press, 1974), grades 6-12. Both Pennant and Argus Communications offer multimedia kits. Merrill Harmin has authored *Making Sense of Our Lives* for Argus. It employs values clarification techniques.[20]

Television and Videotapes

Increasing evidence supports the contention that television has enormous impacts upon our daily lives and subtly changes our attitudes.[21] Interestingly, the debate over a program such as *Sesame Street* is not whether or not it makes a difference, but rather whether it is making too much of a difference in favor of upper-class children.

If you wish to relate television programs to your educational situation, you can write for the "Teacher's Guide to Television," Box 564, Lenox Hill Station, New York, New York 10021, for a bulletin which alerts you to coming network specials.

The Agency for Instructional Television, Box A, Bloomington, Indiana 47401, coordinates the efforts of the educational consortium, which has produced several series directed at emotional and social problems. One series, *Inside/Out,* is a series of thirty fifteen-minute color programs for eight to twelve year olds which raise a dilemma and leave it unsolved. The topics covered include practical joking, moving, divorce, and death. A second series, for eleven to thirteen year olds, is called *Self-Incorporated.* It centers more on dating, peer pressures, and achieving. Two others are titled *Bringing It All Back Home* and *Ripples.*

Through film distributing companies, it is possible to get television programs. The CBS series on American Blacks is one example. Occasionally special groups will produce televison programs. The National Council of Churches developed a program, *The Filthy Rich,* which pursued the question "What are personal and corporate resonsibilities in regard to the environment?"

Film/Film loops/Filmstrips/Slides

The advent of film in the early twentieth century produced a rash of predictions that classrooms would soon be radically transformed into learning centers from which it would be difficult to remove students. What happened?

The simple answer is that film, here used in its widest possible meaning, does not guarantee magical results. Some researchers are even suggesting that it is being overused.[22] As Romiszowski suggests, film should be used when no other medium can as effectively demonstrate a process, reveal information, or convey a feeling. A chief disadvantage of 16 mm films and filmstrips is that they are not as convenient to stop for discussion as are some other media. They are subject to breakdown and, of course, some teachers are reluctant to use film. But when done well, film can provide a clear exposition of a topic and build interest in a topic.

For sources which describe when and how to use film, consult Schrank, *Media in Values Education,* pp. 127–31; Richard A. Lacey, "Seeing with Feeling: Film in the Classroom," (1972) ED 062 762; and Richard A. Maynard, "The Celluloid Curriculum: How to Use Movies in the Classroom," (1971) ED 061 211. An extensive listing of films is Jane Cushing, *101 Films for Character Growth* (Notre Dame, Indiana: Fides, 1969).

If you wish to explore methods for student production of film, see Stuart Roe and Elaine Corbeil, "Getting Into the Creativity Thing," *Today's Filmmaker* 4, no. 3 (February 1975): 24+; and Cynthia Whitcomb, "The Making of Sam Speed, Super Sleuth . . ." *Learning* 2, no. 2 (November 1974): 24–29. Especially helpful for secondary students are the instructions for story-boarding given by Jerold Kemp, *Planning and Producing Audio-Visual Materials,* 3rd ed. (Scranton, Pa.: Chandler, 1975), pp. 38–40, 52–58.

Films

Considering the multitude of films available through commercial firms and regional or state educational agencies, it would be hopeless to list specific film titles. The books cited earlier summarize the films' central points. Many could be used with at least several of the approaches described in the previous chapters.

Some films employ special techniques to make a quick penetrating statement about society. The classic is Charles Braverman's *American Time Capsule,* a three-minute collage of still illustrations which depict the nation from Revolutionary days through the 1950s. Some of the illustrations are military and political. The dizzying pace nevertheless allows you to react and promotes discussion. The film is available from Pyramid Films.

Another approach is to use clips from famous movies to build discussions. A prime example is the Learning Corporation of America series *Searching for Values: A Film Anthology* (1972), which uses excerpts from "On the Waterfront" and other dramatic movies. Guides with the films and the narrator's segments usually are structured toward a "right" answer.

Also somewhat burdened with a "right" answer approach are thematic films. At the primary level, the Ealing Company has a series of 8 mm films which present problem situations. They are designed to help children become aware of the values which guide their behavior. Titles of two of the four-minute films are "The Borrowed Bicycle" and "The Cashier's Mistake." CRM/McGraw-Hill Films has a set of films entitled *Conflict and Awareness* for senior high students. Individual films cover such themes as homosexuality, frustration, suicide, and group conformity.

A number of films attempt to take a simple concept and build a short situation around it which will prompt discussion. Typical is the Bailey series for primary, intermediates, and juniors, entitled *Understanding Ourselves* and *Understanding Others.* Concepts include cooperation ("The Glass Marble"), friendship, and decision making.

One final point—as Schrank indicates, film companies have certain styles and approaches which they favor. Don't write off values films because of an initial bad experience. If you wish to use films which do have a stated ethical position, for example, you might be attracted to those produced by the Paulist Productions. At the secondary and adult level, they have the "Insight" films and at the elementary level they offer the *Bloomin' Human* series.

Film loops

Universal Education and Visual Arts of New York have produced a series of three-minute Super 8 mm film loops (silent) which are highly

popular with elementary children. Typically they show cartoon characters in the midst of a conflict situation which then closes with the
question, "What will happen and why?" Some titles include: "Let's Talk
About . . . Being Mean!" "Let's Talk About . . . Procrastination!" and
"Let's Talk About Flying Off the Handle!" "Exploring Moral Values,"
forty-four dramatized situations designed by Louis Raths for grade
levels 2–6, is also available as a silent Super 8 mm film loop from Schloat
Productions. The situations ask the student to answer the question,
"What would I do in this situation?"

Filmstrips

Because of the economy which must be employed in films in closely
coordinating picture and script, and the relatively low cost of producing
filmstrips, many advocates of the various values education approaches
have produced filmstrips which are directly related to their approach.
Some commercial companies have produced filmstrips which border on
several approaches.

Filmstrips can be effectively stopped and started to facilitate discussion. They share with film loops a relatively simple operation.

One highly praised publishing company is Guidance Associates. A
number of their filmstrip sets are for the lower grades, especially K-4.
"But It Isn't Yours," "First Things," and "Social Reasoning" are strips
which employ Kohlberg's approach to moral reasoning.

Schrank, who rated Guidance Associates highly, also wrote in glow-
ing terms of the filmstrips made by the Thomas S. Klise Company. Their
abstract experiments with colors and shapes would place them in the
evocation camp.

"Developing Basic Values" is an intermediate set of filmstrips from
the Society for Visual Education. Topics covered include property rights
and consideration for others, which would reflect the transmission approach. Similarly, Eye Gate offers sets for the kindergarten and primary
levels, such as "Furthering Values," "Values," and "Understanding Values" (I, J), which focus on traditional value themes such as stealing,
kindness, politeness, and responsibility. Students are supposed to exercise personal choice after seeing a situation.

Parents' Magazine Films, Inc., has produced "Growing Up with Values," a two-set unit for intermediate grades, which were made in conjunction with the Erikson Institute for Early Education. The approach
used seems consistent with the moral reasoning and integration typologies.

The Schloat organization has a number of filmstrips for grades 2–6.
Raths was the consultant for some, and the values clarification approach
is obvious. Also for the same age level is the Winston Press release
"Values in Action." Situations are presented which teachers have noted

in classrooms. Students role-play their solutions. Juniors can also benefit from using this set, which was built upon the work of Shaftel and Shaftel, and which is more likely to be in the integration approach.

Argus Communications, Pathescope, and Pennant also have selections which would reflect the values clarification approach. The Argus filmstrip "Strike it Rich" would be useful with juniors through adult.

Slides

Clearly the leading producer of slides sets related to values discussions is The Center for Humanities, White Plains, New York. Most frequently, they package two carousels of slides as one program and make it available with a cassette or record text. An advantage of slide sets is that you can stop the program for interaction or remove the slides for showing as individual focal points. One of the chief disadvantages is that the slide sets are relatively expensive.

The topics which the Center has explored include the relation of science and religion, an introduction to values clarification, the role of film as a conveyor of societal values, and religious organizations from colonial times to the present. Frequently works of art are used as slide subjects. Some sets seem to have definite value stances themselves; but on whole, these sets are quite good for senior high and collegiate students.

Mentioned earlier was the Sandak Company, a specialty firm which is commissioned by many museums to take the "official" portraits of their paintings. Sandak sells individual slides and sets on a variety of topics.

Simulation Games

> The term "game" connotes fun. And activities that are fun seem to be incompatible with activities that are serious. . . .
>
> A game is essentially a simplified slice of reality. Its structure reflects a real-world process that the designer wishes to teach or investigate; the game serves as a vehicle for testing that process or for learning more about its working. . . .
>
> In playing games, students tend to develop feelings of effectiveness and control, because the actions they take in the game produce results.[23]

Some students are more likely to honestly share their feelings in games than in paper-pencil tests.[24] The chief disadvantages of using simulations is that they take a long time, they tend to be expensive, and they are difficult to evaluate.

An excellent introduction to game organization and general resources for the beginner is Mark Heyman, *Simulation Games for the Classroom* (Bloomington, Indiana: Phi Delta Kappa Educational Foundation, 1975). This booklet, part of the Kappan "fastback" series, details more pros and cons of gaming and helps you determine when and when not to use games. Another good reference for brief discriptions of the major commercial games is Philip H. Gillispie, *Learning Through Simulation Games* (New York: Paulist Press, 1973). A more technical book is G. I. Gibbs, *Handbook of Games and Simulation Exercises* (Beverly Hills, Calif.: Sage Publications, 1974), an excellent reference. The same organization has another reference, C. Greenblat and R. L. Dukes (eds)., *Gaming-Simulation: Rationale, Designs, and Applications* (1975).[25]

If you decide that simulation games do mesh with your educational philosophy and will be compatible with your values education approach (they seem to be particularly appropriate for the transmission, integration, action, and investment approaches), you still should be very careful when you consider making a game or having students make a game. One good set of guidelines for using games is Rice, "Games Are More than Gimmicks."[26]

Feel free to try out gaming and use the references cited to familiarize yourself with the tremendous resources available. If you still are hesitant about going on your own, and wish to try out some games which seem to be particularly appropriate for values, I would recommend these:

Psychology Today has produced a series of board/card games which have values implications. In particular, *Body Talk, Black and White,* and *Woman and Man* are useful as introductory games. They can be played in a short time. *Body Talk* encourages players to use their gestures and body movements to more openly express their feelings. *Black and White* is supposed to convey the feelings of a minority group. It could as easily be entitled *Rich Man-Poor Man*. *Woman and Man* "loads the dice" in favor of the players taking male roles, and is supposed to convey to the participants the feelings of the female. Both the information given through the questions used and society today make this game somewhat dated.

Interact has a number of games. One series includes *Dig,* which gets good reviews from teachers who have used it. A class is broken into two groups, each representating a distinct culture. Over a period of time they recreate artifacts representing the values of their culture. The artifacts are buried, after being broken. Each group, acting as archeologists, discovers and interprets the remains!

Another skill game, constructed by Pennant, is *My Cup Runneth Over.* The basic idea of the game is to learn to share your values with others through revealing statements.

Continuing work is being done in game research. You may wish to contact the following agencies:

Academic Games Associates Inc., 430 East Thirty-third St., Baltimore, Maryland 21218. Games produced by this group are often affiliated with the work of researchers at Johns Hopkins. They are still working on a game called *High School,* based on the work of sociologist James Coleman.

Abt Associates, 55 Wheeler St., Cambridge, Massachusetts 02138, has made such games as *Empire* which simulate the colonial business world. They are similar to **Foreign Policy Associates,** which catalogs a number of games in social sciences.

Simile II, Box 1023, 1150 Silverado, La Jolla, California 92037 has a number of political simulations, such as *Napoli* and *Starpower.*

Friendship Press has produced a boardgame entitled *Values.* It may be obtained through their distribution office, Box 37844, Cincinnati, Ohio 45237.

Value Activity: "Right(s) or Wrong(s)?"

With a group, build the game called *Right(s) or Wrong(s)*. The game can be easily adapted to fit the group you are working with. If you'll be with a group of students, it can focus on students' rights. If you are more interested in teachers' rights, it can be modified that way.

First you and the group will have to gather accounts about court cases on the topic you choose to explore. From the library, the American Civil Liberties Union, or professional education groups you should be able to find enough leads. Have each case summarized, so you can have the background facts on one card and the finding of the court on another card, or on the reverse side.

Determine a way in which you could have each member of the group draw from a pile of cards and read about the case. Decide whether each one is to give his own reasoning and feelings about how the case was resolved, or if all participants voice their verdicts about the case.

Hopefully what will be gained will be a greater appreciation of the complexity of relations between students and teachers, as well as a greater understanding of the specific cases involved.

Value identification: "Right(s) or Wrong(s)?"

Activity: Participants build a game on student/teacher rights which, after playing, will reveal the players' feelings about the rights of their group and their opposite group.

Learning aids: A set of cards (4 X 6). Blank pads of paper for scoring points.

Unit interaction: Group will do research as described earlier. Sample cases: The Tinker case from Des Moines, Iowa, which involved the wearing of armbands. As each participant researches a case, he or she will write a brief description of the facts on one side of the card and the verdict on the other side. The verdict should also show some reasons why the courts reached that decision.

The group should decide before playing what kind of scoring system is to be used (perhaps five points for each right guess). If a player picks up the case he researched, he must disqualify himself from that case.

Evaluation: (The sharing of feelings about the appropriateness of rights and responsibilities) is more important than the ability to make "educated guesses" about the cases. The discussion should indicate how effective members of the group have been in opening up about their personal reactions to the question of rights.

Suggestions: Another topic could be violence in the society or at school. Or use a simply made game such as *Broken Squares,* widely available, to show how difficult it is to communicate and cooperate without words.

SUMMARY

While this chapter contains a compilation of resources for values education, it has been, first and foremost, an invitation to experiment with resources that can enhance the total learning climate. Media, like other educational tools, are merely that—materials to underscore the fundamental message of caring and concern which you have as a teacher. The media you use will reflect your values and your educational goals for the students with whom you work.

Don't be discouraged by the flood of resources available, even though it is frustrating that you can't keep up with the materials being produced. Don't assume that if you can't purchase the latest equipment, you're doomed to provide second-class instruction.

Remember to be adaptable. You have a lot of resources available, in your classroom, in your community, and through a multitude of agencies that will provide them inexpensively. Be flexible in your use of media so that you can provide the most meaningful education possible for your students.

One final piece of advice—always preview media before using! To go by the description in the brochure or to assume that the filmstrip in the can is the one you want can lead to educational disasters!

Notes

1. Gerald M. Torkelson, *Educational Media* (Washington, D.C.: National Education Association, 1968, 1972), pp. 3–4.

2. From Oscar J. Rumpf, *The Use of Audio-Visuals in the Church* (Philadelphia: Christian Education Press, 1958), pp. 9–17. Copyright 1958 The Christian Education Press. Used by permission of the United Church Press.

3. Edgar Dale, *Audio-Visual Methods in Teaching* (New York: Holt, 1969). James W. Brown, Richard B. Lewis, and Fred F. Harcleroad, *AV Instruction: Technology Media and Methods*, 4th ed. (New York: McGraw-Hill, 1973). John R. Bullard and Calvin E. Mether, *Audiovisual Fundamentals* (Dubuque, Iowa: William C. Brown, 1974).

4. L. J. Briggs, *Students' Guide to Handbook of Procedures for the Design of Instruction* (Pittsburgh: American Institutes for Research, 1972), p. 29.

5. Walter Wager, "Media Selection in the Affective Domain: A Further Interpretation of Dale's Cone of Experience for Cognitive and Affective Learning," *Educational Technology* 15, no. 7 (July 1975): 9–13.

6. John B. Haney and Eldon J. Ullmer, *Educational Communications and Technology*, 2nd ed. (Dubuque, Iowa: William C. Brown, 1975), especially Chapter 4, pp. 28–43.

7. Haney and Ullmer, *Educational Communications and Technology*, p. 29. Malcolm Knowles, *The Adult Learner: A Neglected Species* (Houston: Gulf Publishing, 1973), pp. 45–49.

8. Rumpf, *Audio-Visuals in the Church*, pp. 24–51.

9. The Kodak Company has an inexpensive copy stand utilizing an Instamatic camera. With that camera and stand students don't have to worry about lighting. Carolyn A. Paine, "The Great Picture Lift," *Learning* 2, no. 7 (April 1974): 60–62.

10. *A Catalog of U. S. Government Produced Audio-Visual Materials, 1974–75,* available without charge from the National Audio-Visual Center, National Archives and Records Services, General Services Administration, Washington, D.C. 20036. It contains over 4,500 listings of audio-visual materials for sale and/or rental from federal agencies. An example of a commercial firm selling slide sets is Sandak, Inc., 180 Harvard Avenue, Stamford, Connecticut 06902.

11. Write Hudson Photographic Industries, Inc., Education Products Divsion, Irvington-on-Hudson, New York 10533 for the "U" Film Kit.

12. Helen Fling, *Marionettes: How to Make and Work Them* (New York: Dover, 1973).

13. National Information Center for Educational Media, *Index to 8mm Motion Cartridges*, 4th ed. (Los Angeles: 1974–75).

14. For a model of Shakespeare's Globe Theatre, contact Perfection Form Company, 7582 Hickman Road, Des Moines, Iowa 50322.

15. For details on a host of regional and local ethnic heritage projects funded by the Department of Health, Education and Welfare, write to the Office of Education, Division of International Education, Ethnic Heritage Studies Branch, Washington, D. C. 20202.

16. Edmund V. Gillon, Jr., *Early New England Gravestone Rubbings* (New York: Dover, 1966).

17. *The Family of Man* (New York: Museum of Modern Art, New York, 1955).

18. Otto Klineberg, *Social Psychology* (New York: Holt, 1940), especially pp. 203–22.

19. *In White America*, Columbia Records, 1968, no. KOL-6030.

20. See Douglas Superka, et al., *Values Education Sourcebook* (Boulder, Col.: Social Science Education Consortium, 1976), pp. 68, 152 for other similar resources.

21. Sidney H. Head, *Broadcasting in America: A Survey of Television and Radio,* 2nd ed. (Boston: Houghton Mifflin, 1972), pp. 499–520. Randall Harrison, "The Violent Shows: A Clear and Present Danger to Your Child," *Parents Magazine* 49, no. 10 (October 1974): 32ff. Robert L. Hilliard and Hyman H. Field, *Television and the Teacher: A Handbook for Classroom Use* (Philadelphia: Hastings, 1975).

22. A. J. Romiszowski, *The Selection and Use of Instructional Media* (New York: Wiley, 1974). Jeffrey Schrank, *Media in Values Education* (Niles, Ill.: Argus, 1970).

23. Alice Kaplan Gordon, *Games for Growth* (Palo Alto, Calif.: Science Research Associates, Inc., 1970), frontispiece.

24. David L. DeVries and Keith J. Edwards, "Learning Games and Student Teams: Their Effects on Classroom Process," *American Educational Research Journal* 10, no. 4 (Fall 1973): 307–18.

25. Jean Belch, *Contemporary Games* (Detroit: Gale Research Company, 1973), descriptions of over 900 games, mostly simulations. David Zuckerman and Robert Horn, *The Guide to Simulation Games for Education and Training,* 2nd ed. (Lexington, Mass.: Information Resources, 1973), a directory of 600 simulations, with little more than a description of the games. *Simulation Games for the Social Studies Classroom* (New York: Foreign Policy Association, 1970).

26. Ann Smith Rice, "Games Are More than Gimmicks," *Forecast for Home Economics* (February 1974): 36–38ff.

part three

PLANNING
THE RETURN

Throughout this book, values education has been described as the systematic attempt to structure value issues in the classroom so students can more effectively act on their choices or can more consciously decide not to act. The book has been directed to you, as an educator or future educator, to help you become more familiar with valuing theories and techniques, so that you might feel more comfortable in raising value questions in your educational situation.

Part three is built upon the assumption that you are likely to need and want to modify several of the approaches which have been described for your own situation. Practicing teachers tell me frequently that their budgets prevent them from buying the sets or kits they would like to have. And so they want help in constructing their own values activities.

Chapter 5 details ways educators ought to plan for value "trips." Much work has been done on constructing cognitive objectives, but little of a practical help has been done in the realm of values education. The chapter stresses the characteristics of good objectives and the degrees of difference in values objectives, and gives some classroom techniques which relate to the various levels of affective objectives.

Chapter 6 highlights measurement techniques which classroom teachers might find especially useful in determining the extent of their students' change, if any, in value positions. In addition to citing resources where you may locate standardized affective instruments, it discusses in general terms the variety of techniques which you may employ to "triangulate" value cores which the student have. The chapter encourages greater use of measurement for the students' benefit.

Chapter 7 is the capstone of the book, listing the variety of ways in which value questions could be explored. It opens with comments on the values investment approach, but is primarily devoted to examples of inexpensive strategies devised by teachers whom I know.

Preparing Value
Objectives

The first part of *You and Values Education* stressed that the structure of the school, historically and psychologically, forces teachers to engage in values education. Chapters 3 and 4 commented on the vast array of new curriculum sets and media selections you have available if you choose to confront values education directly.

Even if you were not inclined towards values education, the accountability movement, growing out of general dissatisfaction with what schools have not accomplished, would place increasing pressures on you to carefully plan objectives and activities for your students. And, as has been demonstrated in various needs-assessment studies, communities do want their schools to include affective goals and programs.[1]

Even without this pressure, teachers should be concerned about the individual needs of their students and should take into account the information, skills, and value issues which are appropriate for class presentation. Put in terms of values investment, you can hardly be an effective broker for your clients (the students) if you cannot interpret to them the ways in which they can best invest their potential to gain the most rewarding payoffs, personally and socially.

Perhaps you agree, generally speaking. But you may still be reluctant to work in values education perhaps because of the following reasons. It may be too sensitive or controversial. You may think it impossible to convert abstract goals into concrete objectives. You may have to show results in cognitive knowledge gained and may be leery about valid documentation of affective change. Or you may feel you would be losing spontaneity, or worse, manipulating your students.

I cannot offer simple answers to these real problems. I do not profess to be able to give you a system which will guarantee 100 percent satisfactory results.

But imagine this situation. It is the last day of class. The students are about to be dismissed. As you glance at your young scholars for the last time, you realize that they are *exactly the same* as they were the first day you met them. Off-hand you can see no differences in their behavior from that first session. Would you be content to have that happen to you?

I believe it would be the rare educator who does not want to see *some* kind of change in his or her students. That does not mean radical change, necessarily. With some learners, you can recognize from the glow in their eyes that they have affirmed the standards they already held, but with new information. Or you may feel good when a student enthusiastically demonstrates a hard-won skill. At times, usually those unexpected moments, you may feel fulfilled when a student quietly recalls a discussion and informs you he is thinking of changing his career objectives.

The point is that *if* you are concerned about changes in your students, you should think about the *type* of changes you want. I suspect some of them will be related to values. In this chapter I encourage you to plan more directly *for yourself and your students* what values you wish to confront. And after you draw up your plans, you can turn them into clear *objectives* for your students. I also suggest alternative routes by which you *both* can learn what changes have developed and which objectives have been met.

Numerous books have been written telling teachers how to design objectives. Virtually all of them concentrate upon the cognitive or "intellectual" domain. The best known include R. F. Mager, *Preparing Instructional Objectives* (Palo Alto, California: Fearon, 1962); Robert Kibler, et al., *Behavioral Objectives and Instruction* (Boston: Allyn & Bacon, 1970); and Norman Gronlund, *Stating Behavioral Objectives for Classroom Instruction* (New York: Macmillan, 1970).

For a more specific look at affective objectives and related problems, consult *Issues in Measuring Teacher Competence for Affective Education,* ED 065 554. See also Daniel Tanner, *Using Behavioral Objectives in the Classroom* (New York: Macmillan, 1972), pp. 37–71; and Alfred S. Forsyth, Jr., *Toward Affective Education: A Guide to Developing Affective Learning Objectives* (Columbus, Ohio: Battelle Memorial Institute, 1973).

WHAT ARE GOOD OBJECTIVES?

Let's begin with the definition of an objective. Simply put, an *objective* is a clear description of some student activity which can be measured or observed in an educational context. During the course of a semester or year, you're likely to ask students to accomplish a large number of objectives. It is important that you attempt to understand the wide range of objectives that you assign.

Domains and Taxonomies

Researchers concerned about the teaching–learning process have developed handbooks which indicate that most objectives will fall into three categories.[2] Most likely a majority of your objectives will be in the cognitive domain. You will ask students to recall dates and theories, explain concepts in their own words, provide new examples of theses, and compare and contrast various points of view. These are *cognitive objectives.*

You will probably have some objectives which would be classified as *affective.* If you hope students will gain a greater appreciation of your subject matter, if you wish them to become more tolerant of a different point of view, or if you attempt to help them build better self-concepts, you are working in the affective domain.

The psychomotor domain is the third area. Typically it involves some type of coordination of motor skills. Teaching students how to write, how to master a swimming stroke, or how to drive a car would be labeled *psychomotor objectives.*

Within each of these domains is a hierarchy of objectives. Memorizing a date in history is less complex than rephrasing a scientific theory. Becoming actively involved in a drama club is considered a more complex behavior than initial awareness of the power of a theatrical performance. Learning how to do a simple carburetor repair is less demanding than learning how to do a complete overhaul. An organization of objectives from the least difficult to the most difficult, or from the simplest to the most complex, is called a *taxonomy.*

It is important for you to build a general framework (or philosophy) regarding your student objectives. Do you have objectives from all three domains? Within each domain, do you have some lower level and some higher level objectives? My feeling is that you should develop a well-rounded set of objectives.

Characteristics of Good Objectives

What is more important is that you prepare objectives which are meaningful, regardless of level or domain. Here are some guidelines. Good behavioral objectives:

1. *Use action verbs.* The key word in an objective is the verb. Such verbs as "to know," "to understand," or "to learn," will leave you and the student in the dark. "To understand" could mean to identify a principle, to give an original example, to state a concept, to identify an error in procedure.

Carefully consider your verb choice. Some manuals of objectives ask the teacher to use the following format in stating their objective: "The student will be able to . . . (verb)." I prefer to state it more succinctly: "The student constructs." Table 5–1 shows a sample of active verbs,[3] many of which can be applied to the affective domain.

2. *Focus on the student, not the teacher.* Remember that it is the student's behavior which is to be specified, not the instructor's. The objective "The student reads the fourteen chapters assigned" says very little about a change in student behavior; it actually reflects the teacher's outline.

3. *Contain only one behavior change.* A clear objective has a singular task or goal in mind. To ask in one objective for the student *to know and practice* rules of good sportsmanship of the local swimming pool is poor on at least two counts. First of all, it assumes that knowing always

accepts	differentiates	praises
appreciates	directs	predicts (future
argues	discriminates	choices)
categorizes	exhibits	questions
charts	forms	records favorite
chooses to	gives example of	reorders
collects	interacts	reports choice
completes	lists	shares
compliments	locates	solves
composes original	modifies	touches
contrasts	pantomines	traces
creates	permits	volunteers
designs	petitions	writes

Table 5–1   *Verbs*

prompts correct action. Second, it asks the observer to find some way to measure the two objectives simultaneously.

4. *Are realistic about the education environment.* To ask for a major value change in one week or even one year may mean the teacher is foolish or arrogant or blind. To expect the first-grader to comprehend what many fifth-graders have difficulty grasping is also unrealistic. Remember to keep in mind how long you will be working with the students, and what their initial developmental stages indicate.

5. *Are observable in an educational context.* One of the most difficult aspects of writing affective objectives is that many of the desired behaviors will not be exhibited in school. Students are extremely talented at picking up the clues about the behavior they know adults want, and will, depending on age levels, be more or less inclined to give back the behavior requested at a superficial level. If your objective is the student's increased "respect for his family's privacy," you build in a condition which will be difficult to measure.

6. *Suggest a way to measure the outcome.* A good objective will specify the manner of evaluation, implicitly or explicitly. This objective from a biology class is very specific: "Given a line drawing of a dog's spleen and attached structures, the student will label the blood vessels, and spell them with 100 percent accuracy."

While affective objectives may not always be that specific, don't be satisfied with such objectives as "The student displays curiosity." This would be more acceptable: "The student composes an original poem about a value or contribution of an ethnic group other than his or her own."

7. *Make clear the behavior expected to the student or an outside observer.* You may not agree that it is necessary to share these objectives with the students, but I believe that students like to know an instructor's intentions.

In sum, the objective should be clear to anyone who reads it—students, their parents, school administrators, and you!

For the next few minutes, try your hand at modifying the objectives in Table 5–2. The first column states the objective which should be amended. For the first five, the second column indicates the chief flaw, based on the seven criteria for a good objective. The third column restates the objective in a better form. The last five objectives are left for you to do.

If you want additional practice correcting faulty objectives and doing it from a perspective different from that described here, see Robert G. Packard, *Education and Teaching.*[4]

Objective and grade level	Flaws and questions	Revised objective
1. Understands the Constitution (grade 7)	Criterion #1—poor verb	Writes a 100-word report based on the Constitution on the rights students have in their school paper.
2. Listen to criticism and change inappropriate actions (grade 7)	Criterion #3—what is being promoted? Criterion #2—appropriate for whom?	After viewing a filmstrip with a moral dilemma, student explains his understanding of what is fair.
3. Develops positive feeling of love for family members (senior high)	Criterion #5—non-school context. Is this the goal of school?	Draws a picture of family members depicting feelings they have for each other.
4. Is able to define *reinforcement* (college)	Criterion #6—no evaluation instrument. Is it oral or written?	From a list of case studies, the student chooses the one best describing reinforcement.
5. Thinks creatively (all ages)	Criterion #7—unclear. Thinks creatively about what?	Designs a new method to test an hypothesis about osmosis.
TRY ITEMS 6–10 ON YOUR OWN.		
6. Has an opportunity to develop self-concept (primary)		

Objective and grade level	Flaws and questions	Revised objective
7. Prefers reading newspaper to watching TV (junior high)		
8. Compares his or her ethical standards to those of a person in a reading assignment. (senior high)		
9. Makes a firm decision about teaching as a career. (senior high)		
10. Forms judgments as to the major directions in which America should move.		

Table 5–2

Chief flaws: 6: (#2—teacher oriented)
7: (#6—no instrument; #7—unclear way)
8: (#6—what instrument)
9: (#4—unrealistic)
10: (#7—too general, unclear)

This exercise should have made you more aware of the problems of writing objectives. But sensitivity to the problem should not discourage you. As you look at the next value activity, evaluate it from the perspective of the seven criteria.

Value Activity: "Moving Day"

Source: Ann Meyer.

Americans move at an amazing pace—often from homes to apartments. And many moves cover long distances. All moves, though, have one common characteristic—the person moving is forced to make decisions about what to take and what to dispose of.

Let's suppose that you are moving from a house to an apartment in San Francisco, for instance. Below is a list of items about which you must decide. Mark the item *M* if you wish to move it to your new home, *S* if you wish to sell it at an auction or garage sale, or *T* if you wish to throw it away.

_____ **1.** Your grandparents' wedding picture.
_____ **2.** A usable black-and-white television set.

_____	3.	Your elementary school report cards.
_____	4.	Your first tooth.
_____	5.	Brass bird cage.
_____	6.	Outgrown clothes.
_____	7.	Old love letters.
_____	8.	A high school trophy.
_____	9.	A complete set of original Elvis Presley records.
_____	10.	Wrought-iron wine rack.
_____	11.	A hand-made quilt.
_____	12.	Baseball card collection.
_____	13.	A blooming African violet.
_____	14.	A Polaroid camera.

Value identification: "Moving Day." For adults.

Activity: Through discussion of the results of the moving inventory, participants reveal their values concerning nostalgic and material possessions.

Learning aids: A handout containing a list of items to be considered for the move. Provide pencils.

Unit interactions: Specific directions are given at the top of the handout. These three choices would be the only options the first time they mark the list. Time: around fifteen minutes.

Evaluation: Class discussion. Main question is on the balance of nostalgic and material possessions.

Suggestions: Ask participants if the decision would be at all changed if they were moving to London? to the South? near their current address?
Modify game: Add another option, *G,* for giving items away. Depending on time available, many other items could be added.

Ask yourself if the educator who developed this activity made the objective or concept clear. How would you amend it?

CLASSIFYING
VALUE OBJECTIVES

Krathwohl's Taxonomy

The most widely known taxonomy indicates that in the affective domain, or what I prefer to call the "valuing process," there are five levels of responses. At the first stage, the learner indicates that he is aware of a new stimulus. The student *receives* new ideas, and may begin to pay attention to the stimulus. On the second level, the learner begins to *respond,* now displaying more than the token awareness he gave on the first level. Learning becomes involved. A key attitude is interest, expressed enjoyment, and a desire for repeated exposure to the stimulus. At the third level, *valuing*, the student shows serious commitment. He joins teams, wishes to practice, and supports the organization. At the fourth level, the student systematizes his beliefs about the *organization*. He is able to defend why he belongs to the organization or participates in a certain activity regularly. He can compare the rationales of groups which compete with his organization to that of his group and defend it. Within the organization, he will assume a leadership role. The final level of the valuing process is *characterization*. Here the actions of the student have become so habitual that they are part of his lifestyle. The student is remembered by others for certain consistent stands.[5]

This taxonomy may still be puzzling to you. Perhaps a concrete example would help. My oldest son's interest in baseball follows the taxonomy to a "T." Until age eight Ted showed no interest in baseball. During a summer vacation that year, the family visited friends in Wisconsin. Their young son had a catcher's mitt and mask and a collection of baseball player bubble gum cards. Playing in the yard and seeing the cards, Ted began "receiving." After returning to Iowa, Ted started asking if he could have some bubble gum cards. As luck would have it, a teacher he had that next year had a brother who was a major league catcher! Ted was "responding." By the next summer Ted was eager to join Little League. That spring we had begun playing catch after he had received his requested birthday gift—a baseball glove. Ted was "valuing." After several years of playing baseball, and feeling some of the pressures of not being the most athletic member of his several teams, Ted still defended his desire to participate. Ted "organized" his thoughts on the values of baseball. He has not yet reached the stage where he "eats, sleeps, and lives baseball." To do that he would have to become even more enthusiastic about the sport, pressuring the family to see major league games whenever possible and wanting to play a pick-up game whenever he had a free moment during recess or after a meal.

May's Taxonomy

Since 1964, when the Krathwohl taxonomy was published, there have been several unsuccessful efforts to have it instituted in teacher in-service programs and in a variety of texts on methods of teaching. Probably the difficulty of dealing with the affective domain is more the reason for its lack of widespread adoption than the taxonomy itself.

Frank B. May argued in 1969 that he had developed a better taxonomical instrument.[6] He claimed three areas where improvements could be made. First, the affective taxonomy should be changed from intervening variables to response variables. In the Krathwohl model, categories such as "satisfaction," "commitment," and "organization" are inferred states of being, and an evaluator can only guess what is in the mind of an individual. Second, May found that the affective taxonomy was too closely aligned with the cognitive domain categories. "Awareness" (Level 1) was linked with "knowledge of" or recall in the cognitive domain. "Organization" (Level 4) is similar to the cognitive states of "analysis," "synthesis," and "evaluation." Third, May argued that the Krathwohl model pays too much attention to words and not enough to behavior. As an example, May claimed that the Krathwohl model would accept "values clean parks" as an objective, where May would favor the objective "Encourages others not to litter our parks."

As Table 5–3 indicates, May retained five levels, but attempted to make each more behavior oriented.[7] He claims his objectives (in the right-hand column) can be measured on a scale (numerically, low to high).

Krathwohl	May
1.0 Receiving	1.0 Experiment Stage Lo 2 3 . . . Hi • • • • •
1.1 Awareness	1.1 Expression of willingness to try something
1.2 Willingness to receive 1.3 Controlled or selected attention	1.2 Indication that something has been tried
2.0 Responding	2.0 Choice Stage Lo 2 3 . . . Hi • • • • •
2.1 Acquiescence in responding	2.1 Expression of choice between things
2.2 Willingness to respond 2.3 Satisfaction in response	2.2 Indication that choices have actually been made
3.0 Valuing	3.0 Concurrence Stage Lo 2 3 . . . Hi • • • • •
3.1 Acceptance of a value	3.1 Expression of agreement with others
3.2 Preference for a value	3.2 Expression of willingness to share an activity with other enthusiasts
3.2 Commitment	3.3 Indication that a certain type of behavior has been shared with other enthusiasts
4.0 Organization	4.0 Proselyte Stage Lo 2 3 . . . Hi • • • • •
4.1 Conceptualization of a value	4.1 Expression of willingness to encourage others to try something
4.2 Organization of a value system	4.2 Indication that proselytizing has taken place

Krathwohl	May
5.0 Characterization by a value complex	5.0 Sacrifice Stage Lo 2 3 . . . Hi
	· · · · ·
5.1 Generalized set	5.1 Expression of willingness to do something despite scarifice involved
5.2 Characterization	5.2 Indication that sacrifices have been made

Table 5–3   *Taxonomies*

Pay special attention to the subheadings. May says that greater specificity can be achieved with his taxonomy than with Krathwohl's.

Sample Objectives

Many teachers I have worked with have had difficulty beginning the task of writing affective objectives. A few examples are always helpful. Again, I would stress that the important point is not how technically correct you are, but whether your objective will communicate successfully with your students.

Level 1: Receiving/Experimenting

Develops an awareness of aesthetic factors in dress, furnishings, and art from cultures under study.

Asks to sample prepared food from several cultures.

Develops a tolerance for a variety of types of music.

Listens to music with some discrimination as to its mood and meaning.

Listens for rhythm in poetry or prose read aloud.

Describes the experiences she has had which relate to the issue under study.

Remembers names of persons to whom he is introduced.

Identifies tools he has tried in the shop.

Level 2: Responding/Choosing

Willingly complies with school health regulations.

Reads the assigned literature options.

Practices the rules of conservation, such as protecting needed plant life.

Assists in organizing several class research projects.

Interests herself in social problems broader than the local community.

Attends one of several concerts available.
Compiles a list of reading books for class.

Level 3: Valuing/Concurring
Feels herself a member of groups which undertake to solve a common problem.
Assumes responsibility for drawing reticent members of a group into conversation.
Designs a symbol for his club.
Writes letters to the press on issues she feels strongly about.
Proposes the formation of an ad hoc committee to study an issue in the community.

Level 4: Organization/Proselyte Stage
Attempts to identify the characteristics of an art object which he admires.
Forms judgments as to the responsibility of society for conserving human and material resources.
Accepts responsibility for his own behavior.
Recruits new members for the school newspaper staff.
Debates with student council members the strengths and weakness of that organization.
Develops a plan for setting priorities for her various extracurricular activities.

Level 5: Characterization/Sacrifice
Develops a consistent philosophy of life.
Announces career choice.
Volunteers for a community post which offers little tangible reward.
Displays safety consciousness.
Risks personal reputation to work with someone in needs.

Perhaps you noticed that these objectives, which came from reference books previously listed, were of a general nature. They did not specifically suggest the method of evaluation, because individual situations must be considered when you use objectives.

Remember that you will be working with students with various needs and abilities. Prepare your objectives accordingly. In most school situations, due to time and subject matter, you will probably be forming objectives at levels 1, 2, and 3. It would be unrealistic to expect that in one term you would achieve major value shifts in the lives of all your students.

Use the following values activity to check out how closely you and I agree which levels of valuing are involved. (The answer is at the bottom of the activity.)

Value Activity: "Your Waste Taste"

Value identification: "Your Waste Taste."

Activity: At the end of this lesson (or unit) each student in this sixth grade class will be able to:
1. State his or her stand on an ecology issue (short range).
2. Demonstrate how he would try to persuade others to take a similar position (long range).

Learning aids: 1. Several newspaper clippings on the Oregon "bottle bill" and a plastics manufacturer stating the benefits of his product.
2. Newsprint sheets sufficient to allow students to write comments.
3. A values continuum drawing of the two or three characters described below.

Unit interaction: 1. Introduce the controversy over Oregon's "bottle bill."
2. Mention this as *one* example of an ecology issue; encourage discussion of others.
3. Introduce a values continuum with Reusable Ralph (who only owns one car, wears one suit until it shreds, puts garbage back on front steps) on one end; Alternating Albert (who one day saves everything, next day throws everything away) in the middle; to Disposable Dan (who uses paper suits, paper dishes, and constantly buys all new furniture and car each year) on the other end.
4. Place clippings on wall. Question: Who do you agree with? Why?

Reusable Ralph   Alternating Albert   Disposable Dan

Evaluation: **1.**   Collect written comments.
   2.   Have students write essay on "My position and how I would get others to accept it." Seal it in an envelope.
   3.   After six months, check to see if students have followed through.

Suggestions: Short range objective: Level 3
   Long range objective: Level 4

CONSTRUCTING YOUR OWN VALUE OBJECTIVES

After all is said and done, as an educator you make the final assessment of the importance of objectives in your learning situation. Some commercial values material carefully spells out objectives for you; other sets leave objectives rather hazy.

Most affective objectives should be tailor-made for a specific educational climate. The packaged objectives which have been presented in this chapter will need to be adapted. Variables in schools are so numerous—condition of the neighborhood, socioeconomic profile of the class, your personality and teaching style—that even within the same building, objectives will vary from one room to the next for children of the same age and grade levels.

Earlier you saw how easy it is to spot weaknesses in objectives written by others. Here are more clues for how to prepare meaningful value objectives.

Types of Objectives

Depending upon your subject area, you might be drawn to one of four general types of objectives. Or you may decide that your teaching style or the specific situation demands the use of another type objective.

Data-Based Objectives

If you teach science or humanities and prefer the values analysis or moral reasoning approaches, you could well decide this technique is best-suited for your work.

> Given (type of evaluation), the student will (type of performance), with (% of performance level) accuracy.

More specifically, a cognitive objective could read:

> Given a series of black-and-white photographs of lung tissue, the student will identify lungworm pneumonia and bacterial pneumonia,

and list at least two characteristics of each type of pneumonia upon which he based his choice.[8]

An objective from a teacher in the analysis school would read:

> Given resources on the status of welfare in our state and allowed ample time for individual research, the student will justify in class debate his proposed short-term and long-term improvements in the system.

You can see that this format is sometimes held to be only cognitive. It is based on the assumption that values should be arrived at rationally.

Action-Based Objectives

For those who favor the action, evocation, and investment approaches, the action model is quite appropriate. The values clarification approach would certainly use it, too. If you believe your class should have discussion, but should move rather rapidly toward some action, you will lean toward this format.

The example used here actually occurred in a community which faced the closing of a large railroad station. The railroad industry had figured prominently in the town's history. At the time of the controversy, it was still an important part of the town's economy.

The teacher was a member of my class and at the time was teaching a freshman math course in the local community college. Her objectives were twofold:

> At the end of this lesson, students in this freshman math class should be able to: 1. affirm publicly their stand on the depot issue (whether to close it, or renovate it as a tourist attraction); and 2. state whether they are prepared to commit any of their own resources to support their stand.[9]

The class session centered on the community economic situation, since a bond issue would be needed to raise enough funds to renovate the depot. Two speakers were invited to class. One represented the "Save the Depot" Committee. At the end of his presentation, he announced that he had brought a container in which members could put their contributions. Also, he brought a petition they could sign in favor of restoring the depot. The second speaker taped his appeal to close the depot. As a local businessman, he believed it would ruin the local downtown area because of the heavy taxation it would necessitate. Both speakers, it might be added, tended to be more emotional than rational.

While action-based objectives are similar to data-based in that both ask for evidence, the action-based is clearly intended to evoke a commitment, on a short notice.

Preference-Based Objectives

A third approach to writing objectives is the preference-based or ques-
tion-based model. If you teach humanities, or if you take the transmission, integration, or values clarification approach, you could easily be
drawn to this style.

Typically, the teacher writes general objectives and uses questions to
point toward the student's preference. If, for example, your general
concern is the "appreciation of literature" and you have assigned your
students novels to read, you might construct your objectives this way:

> Objective: Derives satisfaction from reading.
>
> Question: After you had started this novel, were you more inter-
> ested in finishing it than in doing almost anything else?

If you are more concerned about creative expression you might plan this
set:

> Objective: Student expresses himself creatively.
>
> Question: If you were an artist, would you like to illustrate this
> novel? (Or, how would you illustrate this novel?)

If you were concerned about the carry-over to daily life, you could focus
your objective this way:

> Objective: Relates reading to her life.
>
> Question: Do you feel that reading this novel has helped you to
> understand more clearly why people act as they do in
> various circumstances? How do you think you would
> act?[10]

Students could react to these questions in many ways—perhaps by
informal comments, structured presentations, or a series of written reports. In many respects, such questions are similar to the "clarifying
questions" developed by Raths, Harmin, and Simon.[11] If you are attracted to the questioning technique, both here and for assessment of
learning, see Gillin, Kysilka, Rogers, and Smith, *Questioneze.*[12]

Contract-Based Objectives

With the movement toward more individualized instruction, there has
been increasing use of student contracts.

I have seen the following contract format used in an elementary
school with great success. The affective domain is explained to students;
when they write their own objectives for their independent study
projects, they are to include an affective objective. As the next chapter
indicates, a self-report is the best evaluation for affective learning. Ask-

ing the student to indicate to you some feeling, attitude, or value he believes he will gain from a project is a good beginning.

The investment approach, values analysis, and moral reasoning approach work quite well with this method.

INDEPENDENT STUDY

Your topic_____ Time needed_____

You may use some of these words to help better explain your objectives:

Identify	Explain	Express	Illustrate	(Affective)
Classify	Demonstrate	Diagram	Measure	_____
List	State	Calculate	Compare	_____
Describe	Distinguish	Match	Collect	_____
Define	Observe	Compile	Report	_____
Draw	Name	Display	Dramatize	_____
Contrast	Label	Construct		_____

   I. My Objectives:
      At the end of this unit I will be able to:
      1.
      2.
      3.
      4.
      5.

  II. Projects (Work I shall turn in—paper, photo essay, oral report, etc.)
      1.
      2.
      3.
      4.
      5.

 III. My Resources (reference books, media, persons to be interviewed).
      1.
      2.
      3.
      4.
      5.

Name_____

Values Activity: "Values Display Case"

Kathy Large, an art teacher, developed this very popular and enjoyable activity. Do the activity suggested without looking ahead to her objective. See later if you were able to guess it.

Arrange with a group of your friends or class for each of you to bring a cardboard box or centerpiece dish to class. To meet the minimum requirements you may combine several small boxes, such as shoe boxes.

Step 1.   Combine or cut away cardboard to section boxes and make shelves. Glue and pins are used.

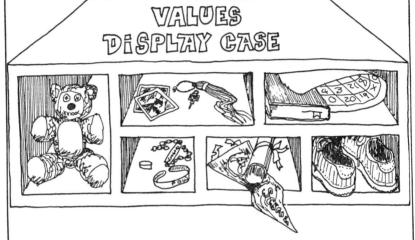

Figure 5–2   *Values Display Case*

Step 2.   Paint or cover the exposed cardboard, using tempera paint, foil, cloth, cellophane, tissue, etc. The colors selected should (and probably will) be your favorites.

Step 3.   Put mementos into box or dish. Include magazine cutouts, snapshots, game programs, ticket stubs, small objects, newspaper clippings, etc.

Step 4.   The box should have a *variety* of sizes, shapes, textures, and most importantly, depths. . . . Members of the group should bring their boxes to the meeting place covered. Have one person uncover all the boxes. Then everyone is to see if they can match boxes and personalities.

Value identification: "Display Case."

Activity: Through the construction of a personality box, students are to reveal some of their values.

Learning aids: As described.

$\mathbf{U}$nit interaction: As described.

$\mathbf{E}$valuation: Discussion follows. How easy was it to guess the group members' identities through the boxes? Did certain items give the best clues? Have individuals comment on what they learned about themselves.

$\mathbf{S}$uggestions: One alternative is to have each student make a values basket. Small souvenirs at home can be put into a flower basket to make an interesting centerpiece.

SUMMARY

Don't make more of value objectives than you have to. Objectives can help you and your students plan more clearly what investments should be made. Never feel required to follow one model or that if the objective isn't perfect it must be wrong. Use objectives as tools to increase the payoff for the students and yourself.

Notes

1. Reports from Needs Assessment Conferences carried out by Iowa State University in conjunction with the Phi Delta Kappa Educational Fraternity, 1975 and 1976. See also James L. Navara, "A Proposal to Assess the Needs of Students in Ten School Districts. Final Report," ED 110 756. This study was conducted in Missouri in 1975.

2. The pioneering works in this field are Benjamin S. Bloom, ed., *Taxonomy of Educational Objectives Handbook I: The Classification of Education Goals, Cognitive Domain* (New York: McKay, 1956); and David R. Krathwohl, Benjamin S. Bloom, and Bertram B. Masia, *Taxonomy of Educational Objectives Handbook II: The Classification of Educational Goals, Affective Domain* (New York: McKay, 1964). The third volume, on psychomotor objectives, was never published.

3. Norman Gronlund, *Stating Behavioral Objectives for Classroom Instruction* (New York: Macmillan, 1970), pp. 53–56.

4. Robert G. Packard, *Education and Teaching* (Columbus, Ohio: Merrill, 1974), pp. 139–60.

5. Robert J. Kibler, Larry L. Barker, and David T. Miles, *Behavioral Objectives and Instruction* (Boston: Allyn & Bacon, 1970), pp. 186–87.

6. Frank B. May, "An Improved Taxonomical Instrument for Attitude Measurement," *College Student Survey* 3, no. 2 (Fall 1969): 33–38.

7. May, "Improved Taxonomical Instrument," p. 34.

8. This format and example were used by Dr. Roger Volker, Iowa State University, Ames, Iowa.

9. This activity was prepared by Ms. Dee Ann Stults of Creston, Iowa.

10. Benjamin S. Bloom, J. Thomas Hastings, and George F. Madaus, *Handbook on Formative and Summative Evaluation of Student Learning* (New York: McGraw-Hill, 1971),

esp. pp. 230–31. Questions such as these were devised for use with the Eight Year Study evaluation of 1932–1940.

11.   Louis Raths, Merrill Harmin, and Sidney Simon, *Values and Teaching* (Columbus, Ohio: Merrill, 1966), pp. 55–62. Examples of clarifying questions include: "Would you really do that or are you just talking?" "What other possibilities are there?" "Are you glad about that?"

12.   Caroline J. Gillin, Marcella L. Kysilka, Virginia M. Rogers, and Lewis B. Smith, *Questioneze* (Columbus, Ohio: Merrill, 1972). This book has some interesting activities involving interpretation of pictures. A classic text in the field of questioning is Norris M. Sanders, *Classroom Questions: What Kinds?* (New York: Harper, 1966).

Assessing
Value Positions

"Would you mind repeating that part between Good morning students *and* Class dismissed *?"*

By A. C. Kaufman. Used by permission of the Masters Agency.

All too rarely do students ask this kind of question. Yet how many students have wanted to ask it? They did not know what was important, and perhaps more significantly, they did not know what was expected of them.

Certainly the thrust of this book has been that learners should explore value issues and share their conclusions. Chapter 5 indicated some ways you could plan value activities with your students so that, when they had clear objectives in mind, they would know what to strive for and when they had reached their destination.

THE NEED FOR
VALUES MEASUREMENT

Often teachers who wish to measure value positions are discouraged by the shallowness or vagueness of the available questionnaires, the difficulty of establishing reliable and valid criteria, or the amount of time needed to analyze the results of affective tests.

Many conclude, therefore, that values can't be measured or the measurement has to be ignored because it is difficult. Don't fall into that trap. If you believe values education is crucial, then you should feel challenged to produce better tests to help students find out where they have been, where they are now, and where they are likely to go.

Helping the Learner

This chapter focuses on the many ways you can give a learner insight into his or her value positions. Note the emphasis—the student's needs come first. While it may be important for you to know just where the student is, it's more important for the student to have increased understanding of his or her own values.

The chief question you should raise with the individual student after doing values activities is: Do you better understand where you are now? I used to think that the major question is: How have you changed your values? But some of my students reminded me that while change is likely to occur, in itself change is not necessarily good or always desirable. If, after going through a number of strategies, a student determines that he has maintained the position that he had before the strategies were done, you cannot say that is "wrong" or a failure on your part. Examination, not change, is our goal.

Helping Society

Although the primary goal of values measurement is to help the individual, we cannot ignore the fact that individuals function in social groups. Citing a number of studies on attitude and values, David A. Payne suggests four reasons why affective learning is important to assess.

How an individual feels about institutions, social mores, and groups has a profound effect on his participation in the society. How an individual develops emotionally and physically often depends upon his or her attitudes from prior experiences in skill attainment. Occupatonal and vocational satisfaction is based upon numerous affective interactions. Finally, what a person learns correlates highly with attitudes and values about learning.[1]

Popham and Baker stress the last point. They highlight again the importance of values measurement by stating:

> Affective measures may get at the most important kinds of learner behaviors. Given a choice between having a student learn something specific about chemistry in the cognitive domain and having him learn to develop a scientific attitude, there seems to be little question as to which is more important.[2]

RATIONALE FOR VALUES MEASUREMENT

Difficulties in Measuring Values

Those who believe it is futile to measure affective learning raise several powerful reasons for their case.[3] Often there is a large gap between a subject's statements about what he believes and what he will actually do. Critics argue that the only way to really know a person's values is to see that person under stress or in real-life situations.

Another objection is that affective tests are easy to fake or cheat on. Students tend not to cheat on the tests, however, if they believe that they will gain insight from them.

Much is also made of the fact that affective measurements rarely discriminate between interests, attitudes, beliefs, and values. What is being measured?

Critics also point to the ethical question of invasion of the students' privacy. Although it may be appropriate to learn their feelings about citizenship and reasons for learning difficulties, when have we crossed the line into inappropriate investigation of their personal lives?

The options method of assessment presented here attempts to answer these objections, although these questions will never be entirely explained away.

The Options Method of Assessment

I have developed this method after working with many teachers who indicated that they did not have the training or time to administer and score complex instruments. The options method begins with the assumption that a *wide variety* of values activities is better than one or two efforts to assess a value position. It assumes that the teacher and the student both know that a *systematic* effort is required to gain insight into a value position. The options method also assumes that it is best if the student knows precisely which instruments are being used to check on a particular value topic.

Moreover, in practice, the options given the student tend to be action-oriented. That is, I favor those activities which require students to build models more than those which can be completed with a piece of paper and a pencil. I prefer simulations to observations.

Giving students a number of options is consistent with the investment approach, which holds that students need to be advised of the many ways they can risk their capital, and that by actually investing their attitudes, their insight into their actual value positions will grow.

The concept of using multiple measures is not new. Forest rangers in watch towers spot the location of forest fires through triangulation. Crews searching for underwater oil deposits use multiple SONAR signals to find the best rock formations to drill.

As Figure 6-1 suggests, you should approach values measurement systematically. Use a variety of techniques—possibly a combination of value activities and formal instruments. Let's assume you have started a discussion about ecology and/or conservation. Rather than having a class discussion at the end of four value activities, you could have a variety of activities: paper-pencil items, construction, observation. The measurement devices could cover interests, feelings, and attitudes. A variety of approaches will help the students focus on what they value about conservation.

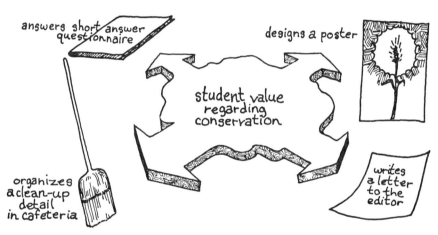

Figure 6-1   *Options Method*

Let's relate the options method to "Careers," one of the arenas of the values investment model. (See pages 168 and 181.) An occupational choice is bound to involve value decisions. Specifically, to help students consider teaching as a career, you can provide several activities that also reflect a number of evaluation modes, as Figure 6-2 shows.

Note that a variety of traditional instruments are used—paper-pencil inventories, observation techniques, student constructions, and to some extent indirect observation. Because these techniques can be applied to any of the five major value arenas in the values investment approach, the many available evaluation techniques will be described in rather traditional categories, beginning with those which require active student participation. (See pages 147–62.)

Before specific measurement devices are discussed, here are some general resources on affective measurement and some agencies involved in values research.

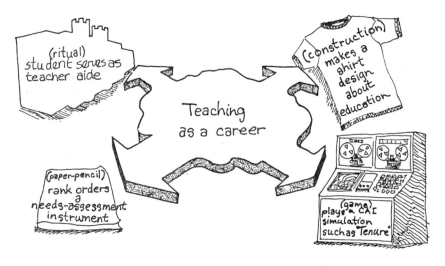

Figure 6-2   *Options Model for Career Arena*

RESOURCES FOR MEASUREMENT

General References

For an excellent overview of the problems of and the procedures for assessing the affective domain, see David A. Payne, *The Assessment of Learning*. See also Stanley and Hopkins, *Educational and Psychological Measurement and Evaluation*, especially pages 282–302; Gronlund, *Measurement and Evaluation in Teaching*, especially pages 323–58; Bloom, *et al.*, *Handbook on Formative and Summative Evaluation of Student Learning*, pages 236–45; Bills, *A System for Assessing Affectivity*; and Brown, *Principles of Educational and Psychological Testing*.[4]

References which particularly highlight the strengths and weaknesses of attitudinal scales include Hoepfner, *et al.*, *CSE-RBS Test Evaluations*, and Robinson and Shaver's *Measures of Social Psychological Attitudes*.[5]

Read Travers, *Second Handbook of Research on Teaching* for descriptions of recent attempts to measure affective responses in the classroom related to subject matter (i.e., how students feel about mathematics, science, etc.).[6]

Research Agencies

Should you wish to learn more about efforts in affective measurement you can write to the following agencies.

American Institute of Research, Box 1113, Palo Alto, California 94302. This organization has worked with the American Institute of Character Education in evaluating their character education programs. Its focus is on measurement techniques other than paper-pencil devices, such as some projective instruments.

Educational Testing Service, Princeton, New Jersey 08540. In addition to doing much research on test construction and validation, this organization has sponsored conferences on evaluation in the affective domain.

Association of Moral Development in Education, Harvard University, Cambridge, Massachusetts 02138. As the name implies, this agency is related to the Kohlberg approach to values education.

National Assessment of Educational Progress, 700 Lincoln Tower, 1860 Lincoln Street, Denver, Colorado 80203. A project of the Education Commission of the States, this organization conducts annual national surveys of the knowledge, skills, understandings, and attitudes of certain groups of young Americans. Of particular interest to values educators would be their efforts to measure citizenship.

Research for Better Schools, Inc., 1700 Market Street, Suite 1700, Philadelphia, Pennsylvania 19103. This organization is making efforts to link the various programs in affective research through the sponsorship of national conferences. It has produced a curriculum, *Skills for Ethical Action.*

Research and Development for Teacher Education Laboratory, University of Texas, Austin, Texas 78712. A regional laboratory funded by the U. S. Office of Education, this group is concerned with teacher performance and preparation.

MEASUREMENT TECHNIQUES

When you face the task of selecting an instrument to help you and the student better assess his or her value position, you might begin with Popham's "four-step generation scheme."[7] He advises that you begin by imagining who possesses the affective attribute the class is focusing on. Then you picture someone who does not hold the value you are seeking or who may in fact be hostile to it. Next let your imagination go; try to visualize the two individuals in various situations. Compare how they might act if they were viewing a performance or taking a test regarding the subject, or if someone else spontaneously wanted them to engage in an action. Finally, narrow your description down to a situation or product which could be realistically carried out and observed in an educational environment.

Consider this example. Suppose your class has been talking about competition. Playing for the fun of it and winning at all costs are seen as the two extremes. Suppose the class decides that they prefer the former. How would you determine that someone in the class truly valued playing for the fun of it over winning at all costs? Use Popham's four steps.

If you accept my definition that a value is a cluster of attitudes or beliefs which generate action or deliberate nonactivity, then you will favor measurement instruments which require some action to be taken or those which let participants indicate they are choosing not to do something. Ask these questions about the instruments you are considering: Do they show allocation of resources such as time or money? Reveal the amount of information the student has about a value topic? Demonstrate how freely and quickly the student responds to a value issue? Encourage her to share written expressions about the topic? Uncover the student's interaction with peers and others regarding the issue?[8]

You will have to weigh, too, the students' background in the value issues you are exploring. If you are just introducing them to an issue, it might be useful to use paper-and-pencil inventories on a pretest/posttest basis. By repeating a test at the end of the term, a student may see how he has changed his point of view. Depending on the length of time you and the class will be working on the topic, you will have to determine whether it is appropriate to assess major value commitments.

Self-Reports

Some researchers have concluded that any attempts to measure attitudes, values, or interests are best centered on personal reports rather than observation. The assumption is that the individual will be the best judge of his or her own values.

Interviews

The simplest method of obtaining a self-report is to sit down with a person and ask him to tell you where he is on a topic. This suggestion may be impractical in light of your class size. Or you may find students aren't willing to trust you with their inner commitments in that formal setting.

If you do decide to conduct an interview, you have several types to choose from. In the *closed interview,* you ask each class member the same questions in the same order. That approach would be favored at the beginning of a term or if you wished to gain a unified picture of the class. Questions you might ask include: What do you want to be? What is your favorite hobby? What would you most like to accomplish this year? What one thing needs to be changed in the world?

The *open interview* allows more flexibility. It will be highly subjective and will allow for a variety of topics to be covered. You will probably need to take notes.

Both types of interviews could be used on a pretest/posttest basis, again, to measure changes in positions.

Diary and Reaction Sheets

The values clarification approach advocates the use of strategy sheets which let students record their value positions over a period of time. Most curriculum kits which use value sheets do not give too many instructions to teachers on how to use these sheets for evaluation.

Without having a formal curriculum kit you can use this approach. Each week have each student fill out a 5 X 8 inch card answering questions the class has chosen. After keeping these cards over a period of time, encourage them to share their recorded thoughts. You can encourage students to look for patterns.

In this day of cassette tapes you might also ask students to tape their concerns once each week. At the end of the school term, you could ask them to review the tapes and turn in their self-analyses of what has happened.

Creative Projects and Constructions

Probably one of the best ways to ascertain the students' feelings is to encourage them to submit original projects or constructions. Creative components which relate to values are a favorite art object, a display of a hobby, a play a student wrote, or a design for a button or sweater (see the following values activity). Or you might ask the student to write a letter of recommendation for herself, or submit an application letter to a college justifying why she needs a college education.

You could give the student a blank T-shirt and have him draw a design which conveys something he values highly. The symbol and lettering should show what he believes he and others need to do about this value issue.

Value Activity: "Sweater Statement"

Value identification: "Sweater Statement."

Activity: Participants create a sweater or T-shirt design which reveals a statement and commitment to action which they want others to take on a value issue.

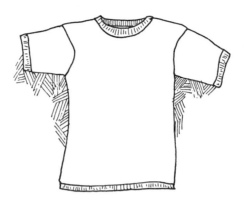

Learning aids: 1. T-shirt or sweater.
2. Colors to draw the design.

Unit interaction: Appropriate for junior high through adults. It is probably best that participants have enough time to think about their value issue. That may necessitate an overnight assignment.

Evaluation: Is the participant willing to wear the sweater? Is the message clear to others in the group? Can the participant easily explain the idea on the sweater? Has the participant actually worn the sweater? "Yes" answers suggest that the participant would indeed hold the value proclaimed on the sweater.

Suggestions: An alternative strategy is the design of a button (similar to political buttons). Or another similar strategy would be to invent a bumper sticker slogan. Actual display of the statement is vital.

Simulations and Real-Life Situations

Self-report instruments are typically useful for introductory measurements. They require high student involvement. Another category of "active" measurement devices contains simulations and real-life situations. You should know your class well before using these instruments. This category is especially useful in measuring student values regarding the rituals of society.

Simulations

Simulations and educational games were discussed in chapter 4. Check the general references on simulations for their advantages and disadvantages. Simulations are helpful for measuring change and providing individuals with insights into their possible actions, but they necessitate extensive debriefing. Research indicates that they can effect short-term value changes, but may not bring about long-term value switches.[9]

Simulations can be "home-grown." One enterprising junior high teacher asked his history class to become a colonial newspaper staff. The class elected the publisher and managing editor. They in turn appointed the features editor, the fashion editor, the weather reporter, and believe it or not, a sports editor! The editors in turn selected reporters. The class chose a specific year and turned out an edition appropriate for that time. The "staff" was subject to the rules of running a paper. Article assignments went through the chain of command, from editors to cub reporters. A reporter who felt too burdened with assignments could only go to his editor, not the publisher, and certainly not the teacher.

After the paper was completed, the class analyzed both the historical data they had gathered and the bureaucratic model they had used. When the teacher suggested that he grade only the publisher and that the grades be passed down through the chain of command, a heated debate on the corporation system of rewards followed. (Incidentally, the instructor finally did evaluate each individual student.)

Role-Playing

An activity similar to a simulation is role playing. Like the simulation, you must do extensive debriefing to find out where students were before they did the activity and where they are now that it is over.

Successful role playing is built upon believable situations appropriate for the audience.[10] At times a teacher may offer a "controlled" role play. That is, the teacher may plant a student who will act in a manner which emphasizes a values question. One teacher coached a student to come into the room noisily, borrow materials unnecessarily, and disrupt other students' work. The class later began a discussion on individual rights.

One issue teachers may wish to test is the "sympathetic bystander" syndrome. Often a group will not respond to a situation calling for action until one person, a "sympathetic bystander," takes the lead.

A word or two of caution about role plays is in order. While it may seem to make sense to discuss a value situation where it arises (by re-creating the scene in your classroom and seeing how students might act), this approach can backfire. Feelings may be so strong that a discussion may put extreme pressure on the "offender." If you're lucky, however, it could result in a "solution." In general, when you search for ready-made role plays, beware of those which suggest right answers without permitting students some range of alternative responses.

The Junior Teacher Activity

If you want to assess what a student *believes* is important in school, you could ask the student to act as a tutor or monitor. Remember, this is not necessarily what the student personally values most highly. The student will probably model and also instruct other students in the behaviors he thinks are important.

Real-Life and Stress Situations

Perhaps you think that values cannot be known unless they are revealed in real life, or under experimentally produced stress. You could make that point by recalling several incidents similar to these. Members of a psychology class in California were divided into two groups, "jailers" and "prisoners," to gain some insights into their attitudes toward those two groups. A basement area in a campus building was slightly modified for the jail. After several days, the experiment was stopped because the jailers had become too enthusiastically punitive and the prisoners were showing too many unhealthy characteristics, including crying, brooding, and violent behavior.

In New York City an attempt was made to measure the honesty of police officers. A film crew recorded the decision of some officers when they discovered a wallet on the street loaded with money and credit cards. When a report was made public which accused the policemen of being dishonest, they retaliated and filmed the general population in the same situation. That film showed a substantially higher percentage of subjects emptying the wallet.

Obviously these experiments raise a number of ethical questions for educators. A major one is secrecy. Another is the appropriateness of such structured experiments for young children, who would not be volunteers.

The following activity is an attempt to take a fairly realistic value situation and have students video-tape their solutions to the question raised. An evaluation of one group who did this activity indicated that it became truly life-like for the participants.

Values Activity: "Values and Video Day"

Value Identification: "Values and Video Day" by James Cline-felter.

Activities: 1. At the start and conclusion of the project, each participant will correctly identify his own value system by completing a value survey instrument.

2. Participants will video-tape conclusions to an open-ended film as a means of stating their own values.

3. Participants will evaluate several endings to a film in terms of the values displayed.

Learning aids: **1.** Rokeach's value surveys.
2. Film: *A Day in the Life of Jonathan Mole,* the story of a Canadian government clerk who wants freedom for himself, but conformity for others. In a dream he becomes a judge determining the fate of others.
3. Video equipment including playback equipment.
4. Props are minimal.

Unit interaction: For senior high, one day's time. Begin with the Value Survey—Part 1 and 1-B. Show the film, but stop it before it ends. Have a preliminary discussion before luncheon break. After break, small groups work on storyboards, script, and tape. Break for the evening meal. Share created endings, and highlight values. Complete two value surveys.

Evaluation: Rokeach's Value Survey—Part 1, Terminal Values; Rokeach's Value Survey—Part 1-B, Instrumental Values. The pretest/posttest use of these instruments, plus the scripts and the actual ending of the film, promote clarification of the student's values.

Suggestions: Select some true-to-life situations which might be concluded via tape. What about the payment of income tax? Equal treatment of all customers? A new housing development which will close a park?

Direct Observation

So far the techniques discussed rely heavily upon the participants sharing their feelings and values. At times you will want to observe the students' behavior against what they have said, because no one is always the best judge of whether he follows through with his intentions, or whether he actually has mastered certain skills.

Observation can therefore be extremely important, although it has limitations. Observations are time-consuming and of course subject to interpretation by different observers. Many observations are done with checklists and in effect are simply rating scales.[11] Observation can be very helpful in the value arenas of entertainment and the public. For instance, someone may say she is not interested in sports or in watching television, but she may unconsciously maximize her actual involvement.

Anecdotal Records

Anecdotal records are systematic attempts by the teacher to record classroom and playground behavior of students. The reporting style is all important. It is easier if you observe only a few students each day for several characteristics. Focus on the behavior the student is exhibiting rather than on the causes and interpretations of the behavior.

You may choose to jot down comments such as "Billie shared his lunch with Sandy" and "Glenda helped introduce Maria to the other students." Or you may prefer to develop a checklist of behavior items to look for. See the reference books cited for sample lists.

Sociograms

If you wish to learn more about classroom dynamics, you could use a sociogram. With the help of another teacher or aide, or with a paper-pencil instrument, you can chart the seating preferences of the class.[12]

Asking students to indicate whom they wish to work with on a project can be helpful in finding out about relationships in the classroom. But this technique should be used carefully to avoid highlighting individual problems.

Indirect Group Behavior

Virtually all the techniques cited so far focus on the individual. Yet individuals become groups, and you may wish to know if the group is acting any different, or if they are holding more strongly to beliefs affirmed before values education. Don't ignore trends of large groups of students.

General School Statistics

Some values curriculum publishers have received unsolicited testimonials which seem to support the effectiveness of their products. In several Texas communities and in Indianapolis, the Character Education Project found vandalism rates and cheating incidents dropped markedly after the program had begun. In Massachusetts and California a program of values clarification seemed to diminish the use of hard drugs.[13] (Officials in these situations acknowledge that there are so many variables it is impossible to say that these programs were the only cause of the change in student behavior.)

The Dropped Letter

To identify group preferences, you might use the "dropped letter" technique. You would prepare a series of envelopes stamped and addressed to a variety of political, religious, and social organizations representating a wide range of views. Then drop them about your school campus. By tallying those letters which are mailed (all come to the same mail box), you would gain a general approximation of the preferences of the people in your school.

Paper-and-Pencil Tests

The most common type assessment instrument in schools is the paper-and-pencil test. Tests are often used when there are large numbers of students or when time is short, because they are considered more objective than other evaluations and because they are easy to administer and score.

Typically, paper-and-pencil tests have the weaknesses of asking for small bits of knowledge and making it easy for the student to give incomplete answers or the answers he believes the teacher wants.

Considering the variety of paper-and-pencil tests you can easily find enough to touch all of the value investment arenas.

Closed (Forced Choice) Instruments

1. Standardized tests.   These tests, which require much research, have been developed in many academic areas and increasingly are appearing for the affective domain. For a more extended treatment of both the available tests and an analysis of the effectiveness of the tests cited below, consult Payne and Redick.[14]

There are a number of tests of vocational preference. They include the *Strong-Campbell Interest Inventory* and the *Kuder Preference Record*. Another is Super's *Work Values Inventory*.[15]

Other instruments which are more general in focus are Allport, Vernon, and Lindzey's *Study of Values, A Scale for Measuring the Dominant Interests in Personality*, 3rd ed. (SV); Bill's *Index of Adjustment and Values;* Gordon's *Survey of Personal Values;* and Thomas' *Self-Concept Values Test* for children ages 4 to 9 and *Differential Value Profile* (DVP) for high school and college-age students.[16]

2. Agree-disagree statements.   This is a series of statements, perhaps quotations from writers in a field or man-in-the-street comments with which the student is expected to agree or disagree.[17]

3. True-false statements.   On issues such as ecology, government, prison reform, or welfare, you might construct a series of statements which require a true or false response. When used as a pretest/posttest, you may determine whether attitude changes took place.

4. Checklists.   Students can indicate their hobbies, acquired skills, and extracurricular interests through checklists.[18]

5. Rating scales.   Rating scales differ from checklists in the type of judgment called for. The checklist asks for a yes-or-no decision. A rating scale gives the student the chance to indicate the degree to which a characteristic is present or the frequency with which a behavior occurs.[19]

Most rating scales offer a three- or five-point spread. The most common form is the Likert scale, which contains options from "strongly agree" to "strongly disagree." As the following illustration indicates, elementary-school children can use a series of faces to respond to questions of preference and value.

	+2	+1	0	−1	−2
School is	___	___	___	___	___
My math is	___	___	___	___	___
My reading is	___	___	___	___	___
My classmates are	___	___	___	___	___
My teachers are	___	___	___	___	___
My classmates think I am	___	___	___	___	___
My teachers think I am	___	___	___	___	___
I think I am	___	___	___	___	___

6. Multiple choice. This familiar test format may be converted into a values survey instrument. Students can reveal which historical figures they like most.[20]

7. Opinionnaires (and questionnaires). Rather than concentrate upon two or three choices, an opinionnaire can ask the respondent to rank order a whole host of terms, issues, or qualities he or she favors.

8. Semantic differential. The theory behind this growing method of assessment assumes that our feelings about ideas and people are communicated through our language, especially adjectives. The differential states a concept and asks the respondent to mark his feeling on a series of bipolar adjectives. If, for example, you wished to find out how students felt about travel, you might construct a differential that looked like this:[21]

TRAVEL

Good ____ ____ ____ ____ ____ ____ ____ Bad

Valuable ____ ____ ____ ____ ____ ____ ____ Worthless

Open-Ended Instruments

If class size permits, individual responses on open-ended instruments are appropriate, although many of the disadvantages of the paper-and-pencil, closed-choice techniques remain. The student may still write or contribute what she or he feels the teacher wants.

1. Case studies.   On the secondary level, students may respond well when presented with case studies which describe the actions of individuals with whom they can compare and contrast their own behavior. Such comparisons might be placed in a diary for the term.

2. Sentence completions.   This is a simple way to ascertain student preferences over a variety of investment arenas.[22]

3. Distributions.   Participants are given a list of items on which they are to allocate funds. One highly successful distribution is the values auction for use at junior high and lower levels. (See the auction items in Table 6-1.)

VALUE AUCTION

Value activity: "Value Auction" from Combined Motivation Educational Systems, Inc.[23]

Activity: After playing the auction, participant will be able to analyze some of his highest priorities and characteristics of involvement.

Learning aid: Value auction handout.

Unit interaction: Allow sufficient time for distribution of funds, probably overnight. Select a total sum of money in keeping with group's resources. Make clear that bids are to be raised by a minimum figure, such as $100 or $1000. Conduct the auction.

Evaluation: Begin the discussion with questions such as: Did you spend all your money? Did you find yourself not wanting to bid? What does it mean if you saved all of your money for one item? Did anyone not win an item? Did you overspend and try to borrow?
   Did priorities change after you had lost any items? Did you have a tendency to drop out of the bidding if things became "hot"?

Suggestions: A lot of sparkle will be added if you can get a professional auctioneer to join you.

Table 6-1 VALUE AUCTION

Items to be auctioned	Amount you budgeted	Highest amount you bid	Items you won
1. To rid the world of prejudice			
2. To serve the sick and needy			
3. To become a famous figure (movie star, baseball hero, astronaut, etc.)			
4. A project that will triple your family's income this year			
5. A year of daily massage and the world's finest cuisine from the world's best chef			
6. To know the meaning of life			
7. A vaccine to make all persons incapable of graft or lying			
8. The opportunity to set your own working conditions			
9. To be the richest person in the world			
10. The presidency of the United States			
11. To love and be loved by someone very special to you			
12. A house overlooking the most beautiful view in the world, in which you may keep for one year 40 of your favorite works of art			
13. To be considered as the most attractive person in the state			
14. To live to 100 with no illness			
15. To know all about me, and know for certain who I am			
16. A center of learning with all the learning aids available for private use			
17. An audience with the spiritual leader, either past or present, that you admire most			
18. To rid the world of unfairness			
19. To donate $1 million to your favorite charity			
20. To be voted Outstanding Person of the year and praised in every newspaper in the world			
21. To master the profession of your choice			
22. A year with nothing to do but enjoy yourself, with all needs and desires automatically met			
23. For one year to be the wisest person in the world, and to make only right decisions			

Items to be auctioned	Amount you budgeted	Highest amount you bid	Items you won
24. To sneak "authenticity serum" into every water supply in the world			
25. To do your own thing, without hassling			
26. A room full of pennies			
27. To control the destinies of 500,000 people			
28. To live in a world where all people gave and received love			
29. Unlimited travel and tickets to attend any concert, play, opera, or ballet for one year			
30. A Total Make-Over: new hair style, all new wardrobe from the designer of your choice, two weeks at a beauty spa such as Main Chance			
31. Membership in a great health club			
32. Anti-Hangup Pill			
33. Your own omniscient computer, for any and all facts you might need			
34. To spend six months with the greatest religious figure of your faith, past or present			

4. Essays. While you undoubtedly recognize this as one of the oldest forms of response, you should not forget it. Writing reactions to pictures or readings can help the student crystallize thinking about an important values topic.

You may ask students to explain what is meant by common sayings of the culture or slang of the day. What does "Fight fire with fire" mean? Try to gather proverbs with various cultures represented by class members and interpret them.

5. Personal and family information sheets. Many value positions relate to our family backgrounds. While we must be concerned about invading students' privacy, no one entirely shuts out their personal and family feelings when he enters the school.

If you deem it appropriate, consider this survey of family rituals. By looking at such behavior patterns as who prepares the meals, who gets the bathroom first, or who chooses the family vacation, the student may discover what his or her family actually prizes.[24]

Table 6-2 *A Survey of Family Duties*

Instructions: Place an F for father, M for mother, S for son, D for daughter, B for brother, S for sister, A for aunt, U for uncle, G for grandparent, and/or O for other (servant, none) to indicate who usually did this task in each parent's family and who does or will do it in your own family. More than one letter can be placed in each blank.

Household Maintenance

Parents' family			Your family
Husband	Wife	Who usually . . .	
_____	_____	1. sets the breakfast table?	_____
_____	_____	2. gets the breakfast?	_____
_____	_____	3. clears the breakfast table?	_____
_____	_____	4. does the breakfast dishes?	_____
_____	_____	5. makes the beds?	_____
_____	_____	6. takes care of garbage and trash?	_____
_____	_____	7. locks up at night?	_____
_____	_____	8. mends the family's clothes?	_____
_____	_____	9. fixes broken things such as electrical appliances, furniture, toys?	_____
_____	_____	10. takes care of the yard?	_____
_____	_____	11. cleans and dusts?	_____
_____	_____	12. does the family wash?	_____
_____	_____	13. does the ironing?	_____
_____	_____	14. picks up and puts away the clothes?	_____

Care of Children

Who usually . . .

_____	_____	15. gets the children up on time?	_____
_____	_____	16. sees that the children get washed and dressed?	_____
_____	_____	17. sees that the children have the right clothes?	_____
_____	_____	18. sees that the children have good table manners?	_____
_____	_____	19. sees that the children get to school or work on time?	_____
_____	_____	20. tells the children what time to come in at night?	_____
_____	_____	21. sees that the children go to bed on time?	_____

———	———	22. cares for the children when they are sick?	———
———	———	23. sees that the children have fun?	———
———	———	24. teaches the children facts, skills, and how to do things?	———
———	———	25. sees that the children do their homework?	———
———	———	26. punishes the children for wrong-doing?	———

Use of Money

Who usually . . .

———	———	27. earns money for the family?	———
	———	28. selects large household equipment?	———
———	———	29. goes to the store for groceries?	———
———	———	30. shops for furniture and other home furnishings?	———
———	———	31. formulates the family budget?	———
———	———	32. decides how much to give to the church?	———
———	———	33. pays the bills?	———
———	———	34. provides the children's spending money?	———
———	———	35. shops for clothes for the family?	———
———	———	36. plans the savings for the family?	———
———	———	37. shops for the family's new car?	———

Other

Who usually . . .

———	———	38. listens to the other's problems?	———
———	———	39. leads the family in worship?	———
———	———	40. determines the family's daily schedule?	———
———	———	41. decides where the family will live?	———
———	———	42. invites guests into the home?	———
———	———	43. looks after the needs of others outside the home?	———
———	———	44. participates in politics?	———

SUMMARY

Can values be measured? I cannot answer that question with certainty. But if you are concerned about the values of your students, you need to make every effort to help them assess where they are, what they currently value, and where they might be going.

The options method of assessment, while it may not satisfy the researcher's desire for validity and reliability, provides some measure of student values.

There are a number of techniques to use to measure value positions. Try out a variety to find out which ones "really works" for the learners and for you as a teacher.

Constructing measurement devices is an arduous task. But don't give up. From a values investment perspective, you are an evaluator, helping the learner see what his option choices have meant.

Finally, use these techniques as cues to aid the students rather than as clubs to indict them.

Notes

1. Reprinted by permission of the publisher, from David A. Payne, *The Assessment of Learning* (Lexington, Mass.: D.C. Heath and Company, 1974), pp. 151, 152. For an interesting proposal of a new approach to affective measurement, see Rudolf E. Radocy, "Quantification of Affective Behavior," ED 090 265, a paper presented at the National Council on Measurement in Education (Chicago, April 18, 1974).

2. W. James Popham and Eva L. Baker, *Systematic Instruction* (Englewood Cliffs, N.J.: Prentice-Hall, 1970), p. 39.

3. Payne, *Assessment of Learning*, pp. 157–60.

4. Julian C. Stanley and Kenneth Hopkins, *Educational and Psychological Measurement and Evaluation* (Englewood Cliffs, N.J.: Prentice-Hall, 1972), pp. 282–302; Norman Gronlund, *Measurement and Evaluation in Teaching* (New York: Macmillan, 1965), pp. 323–58; Benjamin Bloom, *et al., Handbook on Formative and Summative Evaluation of Student Learning* (N.Y.: McGraw-Hill, 1971), pp. 236–45; Robert E. Bills, *A System for Assessing Affectivity* (Tuscaloosa: University of Alabama Press, 1975); Fred G. Brown, *Principles of Educational and Psychological Testing* (New York: Holt, 1976); and David Aspy, *Toward A Technology for Humanizing Education* (Champaign, Ill.: Research Press, 1972).

5. Ralph Hoepfner, *et al., CSE-RBS Test Evaluations: Test of Higher-Order Cognitive, Affective, and Interpersonal Skills* (Los Angeles: University of California, Center for the Study of Evaluation, 1972). Hoepfner and others have edited two other manuals which also describe the strengths and weaknesses of other instruments, especially at the elementary and preschool levels. John P. Robinson and Philip R. Shaver, *Measures of Social Psychological Attitudes* (Ann Arbor, Mich.: University of Michigan, 1969).

6. Robert Travers, ed., *Second Handbook of Research on Teaching* (Chicago: Rand McNally, 1973), especially S. B. Khan and Joel Weiss, chapter 24, "The Teaching of Affective Responses," pp. 759–804.

7. W. James Popham, *Educational Evaluation* (Englewood Cliffs, N.J.: Prentice-Hall, 1975), pp. 177–79. The remaining sections of his chapter, "Assessing the Elusive: Measurement of Affect," pp. 169–94, are of considerable merit.

8. Payne, *Assessment of Learning*, pp. 155–57.

9.   Constance J. Seidner and Richard L. Dukes, "Simulating the Adolescent Society: A Methodology: An Approach to the Study of Attitudes and Behavior," paper presented at the International Simulation and Gaming Association Annual Conference (West Berlin, May, 1974).

10.   Fannie Shaftel and George Shaftel, *Role-playing for Social Values* (Englewood Cliffs, N.J.: Prentice-Hall, 1967). Another book which describes role-playing is Robert C. Hawley, *Human Values in the Classroom: Teaching for Personal and Social Growth* (Amherst, Mass.: Education Research Associates, 1973).

11.   Gronlund, *Measurement and Evaluation in Teaching*, pp. 307–30. See also Anita Simon and E. G. Boyer, eds., *An Anthology of Classroom Observation Instruments* (1968), distributed by Research for Better Schools, Inc.

12.   Robert L. Thorndike and Elizabeth Hagen, *Measurement and Evaluation in Psychology and Education*, 3rd ed. (New York: Wiley, 1969), pp. 449–54, 653.

13.   See various issues of the *Character Education Journal*, published by the Character Education Project, American Institute for Character Education, San Antonio, Tex., 1972, 1973. U. S. Department of Health, Education and Welfare, National Institute of Education, "Drug Education," PREP Report No. 36, 1973.

14.   Payne, *Assessment of Learning*, pp. 351–73. Ronald Redick, "A Compilation of Measurement Devices Compendia," *Measurement and Evaluation in Guidance* 8, no. 3 (October 1975): 193–202. See also note 5.

15.   Thorndike and Hagen, *Measurement and Evaluation*, pp. 388–94, 684, 685. Payne, *Assessment of Learning*, pp. 368, 369.

16.   Payne, *Assessment of Learning*, pp. 351–73. Bills, *Assessing Affectivity*. Walter L. Thomas, *DVP* and *Self-Concept Scales* are available from the Achievement Motivation Program, 111 E. Wacker Drive, Chicago, Illinois 60601.

17.   A pioneer in this field was Thurston, who developed scales on such topics as attitudes toward the movies. See Stanley and Hopkins, *Educational and Psychological Measurement*, pp. 284–85.

18.   Trudi A. Fulda and Richard K. Jantz, "Moral Education Through Diagnostic-Prescriptive Teaching Methods," *The Elementary School Journal* 75, no. 8 (May 1975): 513–18. Their checklist is based on a Piaget-Kohlberg approach.

19.   A typical values clarification strategy of "values voting" is, in effect, a Likert scale. If you strongly agree, you wave your arm in the air. If you are neutral, you fold your arms; and if you are in strong disagreement, you make a dramatic thumbs-down motion.

20.   Claire Keller, Associate Professor of History, Iowa State University, has developed a series of biographical sketches of American Revolution leaders, some of whom have questionable as well as admirable traits. Students rank order their favorites.

21.   Payne, *Assessment of Learning*, pp. 191–95. A pioneer in this technique, C. E. Osgood describes how the semantic differential has been used for comparison of more than twenty-seven cultures in "Probing Subjective Culture: Cross-linguistic Tool-Making," *Journal of Communication* 24, no. 1 (1974): 21–35.

22.   For numerous sentence completions, see Louis Raths, Merrill Harmin, and Sidney Simon, *Values and Teaching* (Columbus, Ohio: Merrill, 1966), pp. 51–71; and Sidney B. Simon, Leland W. Howe, and Howard Kirschenbaum, *Values Clarification* (New York: Hart Publishing Co., 1972), pp. 163–67.

23.   The *Values Auction* is reprinted from the *"Motivation Advance Program"* through the permission of the publisher, the Achievement Motivation Program (AMP) of the W. Clement & Jessie V. Store Foundation. For further information, please write: AMP, 111. East Wacker Drive—Suite 510, Chicago, IL 60601.

24.   "A Family Looks at Itself," by Roy W. Fairchild, San Francisco Theological Seminary, San Anselmo, California. © Marshall C. Dendy 1965. Used by permission of John Knox Press. A somewhat similar technique is the "family crest" concept cited in many values clarification texts.

CONSTRUCTING VALUE
ACTIVITIES

INTRODUCTION

If you've been waiting for the "how to" chapter, here it is! Most of this chapter is a collection of activities which have worked successfully for educators I have known. Many of the strategies are original, and are credited to the individuals who created them. Some are modifications of strategies you may recognize from some of the more familiar reference books in the field. However, they are included to show how easy it is to alter a strategy to fit a unique situation.

A number of the activities vary from the format which has been used so far in this book. This was purposely done so you could see the independent work of several educators. You should note that many teaching areas are represented. Most of these activities illustrate how practicing teachers incorporate value activities into their regular course assignments, which to me is the way values education is most effective.

When appropriate, suggestions for activities in certain subject areas are added to the strategies used. Look under the **Suggestions** column.

There are some general resources which will prove helpful to the teacher who wishes to build his or her own strategies. A general source is Robert L. Schain and Murray Polner's *Where to Get and How to Use Free and Inexpensive Teaching Aids* (New York: Atherton Press, 1963).

Learning magazine (Education Today Company, 530 University Avenue, Palo Alto, California 94301), has abundant creative ideas every month which relate to values issues, and has also published several booklets which incorporate values strategies.

Books which give several suggestions, in addition to some mentioned in previous chapters, include: Mary Greet and Bonnie Rubenstein, *Will the Real Teacher Please Stand Up? A Primer in Humanistic Education* (Pacific Palisades, Calif.: Goodyear, 1972); and Jeffrey Schrank, *The Seed Catalog: A Guide to Teaching Learning Materials* (Boston: Beacon Press, 1974).

THE VALUES INVESTMENT APPROACH

Why Values Investment?

A universal problem for all educators is the clock. Time can be an enemy for a teacher, for there always seems to be too much to do and not enough time to do it in. Even the most liberal educator (who doesn't wish to structure activities for students) knows that there are only so many minutes and that *some* planning is necessary to get the most out of the time spent in school.

Anything which is significant will reveal careful planning, even if the actual experience takes only minutes to complete. Yet how often does the teacher reveal his or her own priorities, racing through things to get at what is "really" important? Values activities which are used as fillers or only for a change of pace will quickly be perceived as such by the students.

Likewise, if the students know that a typical activity can be done in five to ten minutes, with only a modicum of personal investment (raising a hand in a vote, or making a few marks on a rank order), then he's likely to conclude that the activity is relatively unimportant.

Increasingly, I have found that the most effective values activities, in terms of the impact made in the students' lives, are those which require some investment by the teacher and student. Investment here does not mean a financial investment necessarily, although that should not be eliminated. It refers rather to a commitment—a commitment of time, a commitment of effort, a commitment of energy. A participant may be required, for example, to walk through a familiar experience and explain why he is acting in the ways he is, or to take a risk through a public affirmation; or a group might be asked to make an intensive study of some crucial topic.

Figure 7–1, repeated from chapter 2, portrays the arenas I feel are central to the school student. Those options which I found are most effective in forming investment value strategies are also shown.[1]

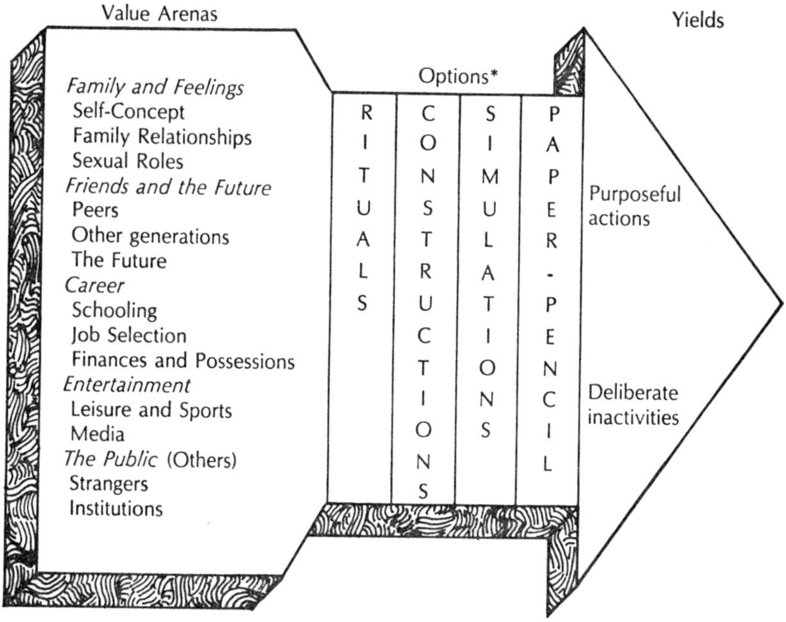

Value Arenas	Options*				Yields
Family and Feelings					
Self-Concept	R	C	S	P	
Family Relationships	I	O	I	A	
Sexual Roles		N	M	P	
Friends and the Future	T		U	E	Purposeful
Peers	U	S	U	E	actions
Other generations	A	T	L	R	
The Future	L	R	A	-	
Career		U	T	P	
Schooling	S				
Job Selection		C	I	E	
Finances and Possessions	T	O	N	
Entertainment		I		N	Deliberate
Leisure and Sports		O	N	C	inactivities
Media			S	I	
The Public (Others)		N		L	
Strangers		S			
Institutions					

* Rituals: Ceremonies, walk-throughs, field trips, laws, humor.
Constructions: Model building, film making, artistic projects.
Simulations: Dilemmas, games, role playing.
Paper-pencil: Research papers, diaries and biographies, value sheets, standardized tests, scales.

Figure 7–1   *The "Yield" Model of Values Investment*

The Yield Model of Values Investment

The Value Arenas

Taken together, the five value arenas will form the individual's personal value system. Obviously, the five clusters are interrelated, but they are separated to delineate certain types of questions.

The first arena is the *family*. Research indicates that one's identity is still learned from the family unit.[2] Although there's a lot of talk about the generation gap, most studies indicate that there is more cohesiveness between family members than the common wisdom suggests.[3] From the family, individuals gain their first impressions of their self-concepts, build their sexual roles, and learn how to express their *feelings*.

Teachers in the primary grades and home economics teachers are probably already comfortable with the idea of talking about families. And teachers in other areas can easily incorporate values discussions about the family. Social studies teachers may ask "Why did the Connecticut legislature pass a law in the 1650s stating that children caught swearing at their parents in public should be put to death"? Humanities teachers and their students can investigate the attitudes toward childhood held by various peoples.[4] Instructors in math and science might weigh the significance of the size of the family. They could study types of food and food preferences or trends in family size, housing needs, and future food availability.

The second values arena is *friends and the future*. As people mature, they grow beyond the family. Friends increasingly come into the picture. Each individual, through these contacts, starts forming opinions about who he or she is, what is expected of him, and what he might do in the future.

Again, the range of activities could be tremendous. Schools increasingly are recognizing the importance of peer pressure, especially at the junior-high level, and some kits are focused on that level.[5] In light of the emphasis upon doing things outside the school, teachers from many fields could use activities based on multigenerational contacts, to explore the goals of the community or the subculture.

Careers are the third value arena. The choice of a career, the third arena, is often based upon the first two arenas. The nation's required formal schooling and the individual's school experiences largely determine career patterns. Closely related to selecting and preparing for careers are feelings about money and possessions.

This arena covers enough territory that educators from almost any institution should be able to think of value topics. Religious educators might be drawn to questions about choice of career related to "service of God." Science teachers may be asked to tell students about careers related to ecology or energy conservation. Some educators will work with young adults grappling with a negative first job experience.

The fourth arena is *entertainment*. The world in which we live is filled with entertainment opportunities. Entertainment includes the press, radio, the movies, and television. It includes our energies spent on recreation and alternate avocations, too. While some educators have begun developing these areas of study, they remain a relatively new field for exploration.[6]

Finally, the fifth arena is the *public*. How we perceive the world around us—strangers, institutions (government, organized religion, civic groups, and social clubs), and the people of other cultures and countries—is a critical part of our personal value system. Because of the growing world interdependence (demonstrated in the energy crisis), students need greater global awareness. Examples will be given of some strategies that explore the "public" world.

Options

The values investment approach suggests strategies which are both active and intensive—techniques which will involve the student.

The first technique is *ritual*. It could be argued that life is made up of a series of rituals. Although you may think of religious ceremonies when you first hear the word, you can think of the many other familiar rituals—the routines of the airline stewardess, the pregame activities at a baseball game, and the series of comments and standard responses that begin the school day.

What do you celebrate? When you're sad, what rituals do you engage in? By observing a ceremony, you may get some insight into what is really important in the lives of the participants. Some schools are now trying what I call "walk-throughs." Rather than have the high school class on dating and marriage talk about it, students undergo a series of experiences that a married couple might encounter—from the wedding ceremony, to shopping for groceries, to having a crisis (the first baby, a death in the family, a partner sent to jail). Paying increased attention to our system of laws and to the informal rules within families seems to give the students greater understanding of their personal and social values.[7] Even a study of humor may be a clue to values.[8]

The second technique is *constructions*—a familiar educational tool. They have been used typically at the elementary level and, to a limited extent, in art classes or humanities classes at the secondary level. Models can be built at any age level. Jay Coakley (University of Colorado) uses an interesting technique when he works with communities who are building neighborhood or "vest-pocket" parks. He provides pieces of Styrofoam, dowel pins, glue, colored paper, and cardboard to the people at the planning sessions (typically all age groups are represented). He avoids more structured tools such as Tinker toys and erector sets. What usually results are unique structures, including some in the shape of gaudy-colored monsters. Only then does Coakley bring out the manufacturers' catalogs, which often contain similar items that can be modified.

One strategy I've used in a graduate class in the history of American education is to assign either a person, a period of years, or a topic, and have the students find illustrations to photocopy to tell the story of the assignment. This technique seems to heighten the students' interest in the subject, reveal the values held in the period under study, and illustrate how selective all historians—the students now included—are.

Artistic projects would include collages, murals, drawings, and clay and paper-mache sculpture, as well as original poetry and drama.

The third technique is *simulation games*, described in chapter 4 on media. The category is meant to be broad enough to include moral dilemmas a la Kohlberg and role playing. The creation or re-creation of a situation from life should let the students ask themselves "How would I react in this situation? Would I go that far? How do I act under stress?"

While I have a personal preference for the first three options, certain times and situations call for the use of *paper-and-pencil* tests, the fourth technique. Not all activities demand an immediate public response. The need for privacy and time for careful scrutiny have to be weighed. The subject may suggest that the unit be approached through an investigation of the lives of people who lived or worked close to the issue. Having students read the diaries of famous people can be instructive. If a primary objective is to help students assess their preferences and how they have changed over time, such techniques as rank orders, checklists, and open-ended statements are appropriate.

Actions and Inactivities: Our Values

The yield model shows that values are not just what we feel internally or even what we say we will do, but what in fact we actually do or choose not to do.

Those who work in education are asked by society to be concerned about values, and yet are hard-pressed to measure value changes. You're frequently not present when the student is faced with critical value decisions. Therefore you may frequently have to infer that a behavior change is a value change. Here are some active suggestions!

Value Activity: Is That Any Way to Act?

Source: Lois Jacobs.

Most of us, when we see something wrong, want to do something about it. Often, however, we remain inactive because we don't know what we might do.

WRITE DOWN A PROBLEM YOU ARE CONCERNED ABOUT NOW.

_____

_____

_____

Below are a number of suggestions for action that you might take on the problem indicated above.
CHECK ONE THAT YOU THINK MAY BE APPROPRIATE. INDICATE THE DATE WHEN YOU CAN COMPLETE YOUR ACTION.

Date:_____

A word of caution: All action should be informed action. Consequently, reading, learning, interviewing, discussing, and generally becoming better informed are necessary first steps before doing something.

Write a Letter

_____ 1. Write a letter to the editor of your local newspaper. People read these columns more frequently than almost any other section of the daily newspaper. You can influence public opinion.

_____ 2. Write a letter to your Representative or your Senators. Washington counts those letters. They really are influenced by the mail from home.

_____ 3. Send a letter to someone in the news who has done something you respect or admire. You would be surprised how lonely it can be for someone who has made the news for doing something different.

_____ 4. Other letters:

Attend a Meeting or Organize One

_____ 1. Contact an organization working for a cause you believe in and ask if there is something you can do.

_____ 2. Scan the newspapers for announcements of open meetings of groups in which you are interested.

_____ 3. Ask your own club, civic group, or church group to have a meeting or invite in a guest speaker on a topic you are

_____ deeply concerned with. Program chairmen are always looking for good ideas. They probably will be glad to let you help.
_____ 4. Other ideas:

Take Part in Some Action

_____ 1. Contact city officials. They are usually interested in ideas
and suggestions from members of the community.
_____ 2. Organize a petition drive. Even twenty signatures could
make news or cause some public official to take notice.
_____ 3. Interview people who are in a position to influence others. Sometimes just a series of perceptive questions can
make an issue come alive.
_____ 4. Wear a button, or put a bumper sticker on your car.
_____ 5. Lead a demonstration if your other attempts to gain
legitimate action are rebuffed.
_____ 6. Other action:

Is That Any Way to Act?

Value concept: How we can get action.

Activity: Make a list of a change you think would improve some
aspect of your community and how you could act on it.

Learning aids: Worksheet.

Unit interaction: See instructions above.

Evaluation: Self-Report. Students will indicate after an appropriate time period if they acted in the way they specified.

VALUES INVESTMENT ACTIVITIES

Sample activities for each of the five arenas are given below. Within
each value arena, one example of a ritual, a construction, a game, and
a paper-and-pencil test is provided. Brief descriptions of other activities
are provided at the conclusion of each arena.

For the educator who is concerned about relating these strategies to
academic disciplines, check the **Suggestions** section for references.

Family and Feelings

Value identification: "Treasures in the Trash" (ritual).

Activity: After participants monitor their family's trash for a one-week period, they will turn in a list, indicating three to five very important items and three to five very unimportant items. To insure privacy, the lists can be turned in without the students' names.

Learning Aids: Cards for the student lists.

Unit interaction: Appropriate for all levels from upper elementary to adult. The assignment should be given with the understanding that this is similar to the work of archaeologists on a dig. The basic purpose is to gain insight into the family's and the community's values.

The points to be made in class: 1. This is not to be an invasion of privacy. Lists might be made on the board to discern general patterns. 2. Areas to focus on: food preferences, toys, other throwaways. 3. An anthropologist in Arizona used this technique in the city dump and found that there were social-class differences revealed through the garbage. 4. Stress health measures to be taken after handling garbage.

Evaluation: Lists turned in by students, followed by class discussion.

Suggestions: Confine the activity to school. Possibly invite in the school custodian to tell what he finds in the trash. One teacher converted this to a math lesson, when his class weighed the scraps from the school lunch program every day for a week.

"Dream Home"

Source: Carolyn Manning.

Value identification: "Dream Home" (construction).

Activity and objective: Each family member cuts out pictures from magazines which show what they would want in their home or what they want it to look like. They glue these on paper, forming a collage.

After completing their individual collages, the family members discuss what is really important to have in their homes.

Learning aids: Scissors, glue, paper, and magazines.

Unit interaction: For all family members. Stress that, if at all possible, everyone should work independently to see if there are "surprises" when family members compare notes. If time permits, the collage could include a rough outline of the house or a floor plan indicating the rooms and features the family wants.

Evaluation: Use of the activity. Does the family request follow-ups from the staff?

Suggestions: If time permits, have the family come up with their compromise house plan. Considerations: cost of housing, ecological features, family roles.

"Marriage Conflict"

Source: Douglas Kachel.

Value Concept: To explore alternative views on marriage and sexual roles (role-play or game).

Activity: After group discussion of story (printed below), participant will present to the discussion group a proposal which indicates his or her personal stance on sexual roles today.

Learning aid: One "marriage conflict" strategy sheet for each participant.

Unit interaction: For high school students and college students. Time required is thirty to forty minutes. Within the group, participants arrange themselves in groups of four to six with approximately an equal number of males and females.

Read the strategy and arrive at the best solution by consensus. After fifteen to twenty minutes, tally results from each group.

Instruct each group to allow each individual to state his or her general feeling about the sexual roles of males and females today.

Evaluation: If something more than a general comment is desired, students may respond to the following set of questions: Is this how your parents would have responded to this situation? If you had children, would you want them to solve the problem in the way you are proposing a solution?

Suggestions: To avoid a "me too" consensus, you may find it necessary to have a "plant" in the group who will take a radical position and zealously defend it.

Marriage Conflict

Henry, age 34, has worked for the United Steel Company ten years since graduating from college with his M.A. in business administration. He has just received a promotion to personnel manager, a job he likes very much and has worked hard to obtain. Recently, making a substantial down payment, Henry and his wife Joan purchased a $50,000 house. Henry is an excellent husband, according to Joan, and a loving father to their only child George, age 5.

Joan, age 28, has been a housewife for eight years since graduating with honors from college with a degree in psychology. During the past two years Joan has taken some additional courses at the local college. Last month Joan was offered a two-year fellowship amounting to $10,000 to attend a prestigious university, full time, some 300 miles from home. This is the only university which offers a graduate degree in her main interest—psycholinguistics. Joan feels strongly that this will be her only real opportunity to develop her own career. She must notify the university of her decision within two weeks.

If you were Henry's best friend, what would you advise him to do? Choose the one answer which you feel would offer the best solution.

1. Have Henry grant Joan a divorce or legal separation immediately so she can develop her full potential as a human being.

2. Have Henry develop a "plan" where Joan could attend the university and return home on weekends and holidays (600-miles round trip) with their son George.

3. Have Henry leave his job and move to the university city, where he could perhaps obtain new employment, but probably at a reduced salary since there are no similar businesses in the area.

4. Have Henry remain adamant, pointing out to Joan that it is her responsibility to stay home and take care of George and the house!

5. Have Henry point out to Joan that while the local college doesn't have a graduate program in her field, perhaps she could major in something else or just take additional courses. Maybe in a few years a new job would come for Henry and they could move. (This, of course, would mean losing the fellowship and a two-to-three year delay).

6. Suggest to Henry that while Joan is a fine woman, you know this other "chick" who has just been divorced . . .

"What's Going On?"

Source: Mary Rushton

Value concept: Identifying some emotions (paper-and-pencil).

Activities: Students will match pictures with list of emotions and situations with pictured emotions.

Learning aides: **1.** Six cartoon pictures and list of fifteen emotion words.
2. List of situations to match with pictures.

Unit interaction: Prepared for elementary students. Would take twenty minutes. Students work individually. Encourage discussion later.

Evaluation: Observe individual reaction on paper. Discuss responses. Do the students understand the emotional terms? What are their attitudes toward the situations described?

Suggestions: A similar commercial set is *Creating Characterization* (Viking).

Pretend you are one of the people in each picture. By the letter A, write what emotion you think is shown in each picture.

Happiness	Indifference	Shock
Fear	Greed	Pride
Embarrassment	Relief	Horror
Meanness	No Feeling	Surprise
Grief	Joy	

By letter B, put the number or numbers of the activity you think the people are watching and hearing.

1. A brother or sister just got spanked.
2. A monster movie.
3. Their allowance is lowered.
4. They saw their teacher fall down on the ice.
5. Their allowance is raised.
6. They see a new baby brother or sister for the first time.
7. Their dad just ran a red light and nobody caught him.
8. Their best friend just told them he's moving out of town.
9. Their teacher has asked for help after school.
10. They've been asked to go to the principal's office, but do not know why.
11. They've just batted a baseball through the window of someone they don't like and they know he's not home.
12. Mom came home before they finished cleaning their room as she'd asked.
13. The bases are loaded and they're up to bat.
14. The worst bully in school is walking toward them.
15. The teacher just called on them and they've lost their place because they weren't listening.
16. Their parents won't let them go to the movie with their friends because the parents don't think they should see it.
17. The T.V. set just broke down.
18. A snake just crawled in front of them.
19. A kid they don't like has just been told he's going to be beaten up after school by three other kids.
20. They've just been told they are going to move to another state next week.

Additional Family and Feeling Activities

Road map   Have each family member discuss where he would like to go over the next five years. Do this individually, and then compare findings.

Family tree   Prepare a chart describing the members of family for the previous two generations. Note if there are certain occupational clusters, residential preferences, etc.

Oral diary   Provide each student with a tape cassette, and let them periodically record their feelings.

My favorite   When beginning a new class, pair up students. Have each interview the other and introduce the other to the class. Have each find out from the other a favorite food, beverage, music, literature, movie, type of party or social activity, way of spending spare time, and gift he would most appreciate.

Playing with a full deck   (A modified version of "body talk," from chapter 4). Using a deck of cards, assign an emotional situation to each card. For examples, an ace might be how you show forgiveness to a family member; a jack could be how you feel when a family member has spoken harshly to you; and a seven might be how you feel when a relative tells you how proud she is of you. After cards are dealt, players take turns acting out their feelings. Other players try to match cards. If the emotions are incorrect, players discard their cards and draw new ones. The first one to have ten cards (five matches) wins.

Friends and the Future

"When We Remember"

One of the most obvious rituals in our society is the funeral, which usually includes some remarks in memory of the deceased. The ceremony, plus the remarks, can constitute a capsule of the person's values and accomplishments in life.

Value concept: The values to be practiced in life (ritual).

Activity: After some discussion about death and a visit with a funeral director, each participant will outline his or her proposed funeral ceremony.

Learning aids: See related books in Appendix A. Random House is producing a unit of materials for death education.

Unit interaction: For senior high and older students. After discussion arrange for a visit to a funeral home. Discuss variations in ceremonies between religious groups and the special services conducted by social clubs.

Evaluation: Participants submit their own funeral services.

Suggestions: Participants can write their own obituaries. Tombstone inscriptions can be discussed. This is very easy to relate to literary outlooks toward death, the historical practices related to burial, and the kinds of items mentioned in wills. Or participants can write their wills.

"It's Nice to Have Friends"

Source: Marlys Dodd.

Value identification: "It's Nice to Have Friends" (construction).

Activities: Following class discussion, the children will show what they do with friends by painting a mural.

Learning aids: 1.   Picture of friends.
2.   Story: *Friends! Friends! Friends!* by Ruth Jaynes (public library).
3.   Poem: "A New Friend" by Marjorie Allen Anderson (Childcraft).
4.   Creative activity: Provide a long sheet of butcher paper, tempera paint, and brushes, and let the children create a mural showing what they like to do with their friends.

Unit interaction: For elementary-school children. Show picture of several small children together in the neighborhood. Say, "This picture shows several children in the neighborhood playing together. Let's talk about our friends in the neighborhood." After discussion do the mural.

Evaluation: After the mural is dry, hang it on the wall and let each child tell what he painted to show what he does with his friends.

"Dreaming about the Future"

Value concept: Participants discuss their dreams for the future of their state or community. There is also a hidden question—how we treat the aged (game).

Activity: Students will share their dreams for the future and reveal, through their behavior, their attitudes about older persons.

Learning aids: 3 X 5 cards, with these *two* messages:

Card one: Share with your group your dreams about the future of your state or community in the year 2000. Be prepared to respond with ways to achieve your proposals.

Card two: (same as card one) with the following added:

One member of your group has been given the role of an elderly person. The instructor will inform you who this is by placing his hand upon the person's left shoulder.

Assume that the person is 75 to 80 years old; that he has had a hearing loss; that he is on fixed income; that he is prone to wander with his thoughts; and that he has some difficulties in moving around.

Unit interaction: Senior high - Adult. Divide the class into groups of five or six. Mark the cards so that you will always know which one in each group receives card one.

Begin by asking what the students generally want in the future. Then you can shift to the second level of questioning about their treatment of the "elderly person." Did the others in the group have a tendency to talk louder to that person? Did they begin to ignore the individual? What about the person? Did he become withdrawn?

Evaluation: Group discussion and reported reactions.

Suggestions: If this proves difficult to handle, you may modify it by having the participants write down what they think the elderly want in the future, and what they themselves want.

"Friendship"

Source: Jane Bedard

Value identification: The meaning of friendship (paper-and-pencil).

Activity: After restating other descriptions of friendship, the student states in his own words the central characteristic of a good friend.

Learning aid: Collection of descriptions of friendship.

Unit interaction: Junior high - Adult. Pass out a hand-out which should provide enough space to restate the meaning of several quotations provided plus to write their own description of friendship.

Evaluation: Open-ended statement.

Suggestions: You may wish to combine statements with posters, collages, and cartoons which convey messages about friendship.

Other Activities

Adopt a grandparent. If students are at some distance from their grandparents, it might be possible to arrange for them to adopt grandparents through a local retirement home or county agency. In addition to visiting them and arranging outings, it might be possible to have them come to class.

Keeping a promise. Puppet shows on keeping promises are quite appropriate for young elementary students. Here's a typical story: You promise a friend you will play with him after school, and you plan to go to his house. But after school another friend says, "Why don't you come over to my house for some peanut butter cookies?" You go there and forget about your other friend. (Source: Gail Gilberg.)

Music and messages. Listen to a recording of such "message songs" as *Conform* by Ralph Carmichael. Discuss what circumstances would make you conform. (Source: John Foss.)

Career

"Something Pretty"

Source: Kathy Large.

Value identification: To analyze what it is which strikes us as being pretty (ritual).

Activity: Students are given a sum of money ($ .25) to purchase something which they consider pretty. They display it in class.

Learning aid: Small amount of cash.

Unit interaction: Students are each given a small amount of money and asked to purchase something pretty for themselves within a week's time. Choices are to be shared with the class. Students can add money of their own to make the purchase if they wish.

Evaluation: Student presentation of their objects. Questions may include "Did you feel under much obligation to find something?" and "Are there certain patterns within our class (beauty aids, certain colors)?"

Suggestions: This same teacher tried a similar strategy. One day, unannounced, she took a Polaroid picture of the class. She then asked the class members to dress up in a "sharp" outfit the next day. The pictures were compared, and comments made on what made students feel sharp. An optional activity is to have students bring in something pretty such as a leaf, shell, or a car part.

"Pennant"

Source: Romola Fritz.

Value concept: The student will be able to share with others in the group some of his or her strong points (construction).

Activity: Each student will make a personal pennant, showing how he has fun and what he does well.

Learning aids: Construction paper, dowels, tape, felt-tipped pens, scissors, glue, and old magazines (with colored pictures).

Unit interaction: Students will be given construction paper cut in the shape of a pennant, plus other materials so they can either draw pictures or cut them out of magazines. One picture should show a way in which they have fun, and the other should show one thing they can do well. The pictures will be placed on the pennants along with the students' names.

Evaluation: The students will take turns telling the rest of the class about their pennants.

Suggestions: Magazine pictures are useful for those with limited drawing skills. More categories can be added, and the shape of the paper can be altered (plain rectangle, personal "coat of arms," etc.)

"Tool Identification Auction"

Source: Rex Stacy.

Value concept: To find out what trades students may be interested in and to increase their knowledge of those trades (game).

Activity: After participation in a pretest and a posttest auction of tools, students will express their personal preferences for these tools and related trades.

Learning aids: 1. Picture cards of tools (available from Interstate Printers, 19–27 Jackson St., Danville, Illinois). Six different sets of cards contain pictures of 761 different tools.
   2. Enough play money so each student is given $100.00.

Unit interaction: Each student is issued $100.00 in play money with the express purpose of buying a new set of tools to use in working in an occupation of his choice. Picture cards of tools to be auctioned will be used; they are given to the student if he receives the bid.

After bidding ends on a specific item and the student receives the bid, he must be able to correctly name the tool before he can purchase it or he must forfeit the bid amount. If forfeited, bids may then be taken again on that particular item.

Evaluation: Pre- and posttest auction, with preference changes noted.

Suggestions: Pictures could be altered for different audiences.

"Choose your Occupation"

Value concept: Build an awareness of possible job possibilities and considerations for junior high students (paper-pencil).

Activity: Participants rank order the fifteen occupations in the questionnaire.

Learning aid: Questionnaire with the following occupations listed: truck driver, teacher, carpenter, store manager, draftsman, production line worker, machinist, farmer, mechanic, doctor, sales person, office worker, small business owner, lawyer, other.

Unit interaction: Ten minutes for rank ordering. Discussion follows on such questions as the extreme positions reflected in the class. Ask "Considering how you are doing in school now, what bearing will that have upon your desired job choice? Are there types of jobs not indicated here which the class is interested in?"

Evaluation: Individual rankings. Keep for diary.

Other Activities

Selling yourself   Construct a list of characteristics which you might use in a job interview to sell yourself.

You and the job   From Xerox Corporation, you can get this simple board game, a game where chance determines whether or not you get a job.

Buying insurance   Find pictures of insurance company advertisements. What kinds of appeals do they make to the prospective buyer? What images of the "good life" do they project? (Source: Brian Kemp.)

Blank checks   Some banks have old checkbooks available. Fill out a checkbook with an imaginary budget.

Entertainment

"Awards Day"

Source: Karl Greve.

Many people enjoy sports. In most team sports, the players assume different roles (even on sand-lot teams).

Value concept: Preference for a role on a basketball team (ritual).

Activity: Participants will choose from alternatives and explain the "award" they would most like to receive.

Learning aid: Handout of "awards": "Mr. Attitude" (team spirit); "William Tell" (leading scorer); "Black Hatchet" (defensive); "Sky King" (rebounding); "Robin Hood" (steals-interceptions).

Unit interaction: Junior high-Senior high. Team members discuss their preferences.

Evaluation: Do this activity before and after the basketball season is over. Ask the squad to analyze the effect on team success if the "William Tell" award got most votes. Will it be a team of "gunners"?

"Auto-motive"

Value concept: Use the design of cars to indicate personal values (construction).

Activity: After drawing the kind of car they would like to have, participants analyze the values it reveals.

Learning aids: Materials for drawing and coloring car designs. A copy of *The Lamp* 54 no. 4 (Winter 1972) (Exxon Corporation, 1251 Avenue of the Americas, New York, 10020).

Unit interaction: Junior high-Adult. Twenty to thirty minutes for drawing cars. Student analysis could either be written (on the back of the drawing), or there could be class discussion, with such questions as: Is this car just for you, or would you want others to have ones like it? It has been said that we don't really use cars for transportation primarily, but for status symbols and toys. What does that mean? Do you agree?

Evaluation: Construction and written comments.

Suggestions: Related to economics and science areas.

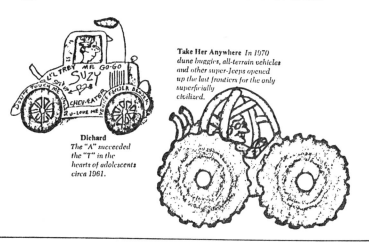

Take Her Anywhere *In 1970 dune buggies, all-terrain vehicles and other super-Jeeps opened up the last frontiers for the only superficially civilized.*

Diehard
The "A" succeeded the "T" in the hearts of adolescents circa 1961.

"TV Producer"

Value concept: The growth and popularity of game shows depicts certain values from our culture (game).

Activity: Participants form production teams which design a television game show based upon a study area (such as math, history, literature).

Learning aids: Collection of games available commercially, such as *Concentration* and *Jeopardy;* or for elementary students, the *Sesame Street* record, featuring the Word game with Guy Smiley.

Unit interaction: Upper elementary-Adult. Most quiz programs are based upon general knowledge which the contestants should know. This is easily related to many subject areas in schools.

What makes the games interesting is the rules and the prizes. Questions which the production teams have to decide include:

1. What skills will be stressed? Recall, putting pieces of information together, acting out information, some physical skill (dexterity)?

2. Do the rules call for intense competition or for fooling someone with answers?

3. What kind of prizes are stressed? Materialistic, feeling of accomplishment, cash?

Evaluation: The game. How playable are the games? How well did team analyze what was important to them?

Suggestions: See games section in chapter 4.

"Entertainment Gallery"

Value concept: People who entertain us come from many fields (paper-and-pencil test).

Activity: Students will bring to class a picture of their favorite entertainers, which will be compiled into a checklist for the class.

Learning aids: 1. Students supply pictures, although teacher may provide magazines. Some students may have sports heroes who are on bubble gum cards.
2. Resource: *Learning,* "From Bubble Gum to Biographies" **1,** no. 3 (November 1972): 61–65.

Unit interaction: Allow time for class members to collect pictures. Post them on a bulletin board for several days. If necessary, have students supply brief biographies of their favorite entertainers. Then prepare a list of the entertainers and have all participants check those they admire.

Questions for discussion to the individuals: Is this a person you would like to be like? In your free time do you engage in the same activity as your favorite entertainer? What qualities does your entertainer possess which attracted you (a skill, courage, fun-loving, humor)?

Questions to the group: What fields are predominant (sports, music, arts)? How many students included family members?

Evaluation: Picture sets and student comments.

Other Activities

Commercial cut-up.   From local radio and television stations get old commercial scripts and films. Edit them to reflect how you think they could be presented better.

Mileage pie.   Draw a circle and divide it into the pieces which reflect your travel. What portions of it are driving to work, pleasure trips (vacations, visits to relatives, and sight-seeing), and business trips (grocery shopping)? If you had to reduce your car travel by one-third, how would you redivide the pie? (Source: Rex Stacy.)

The Four-Day Work Week. If you only had to work four days a week, what would you do in the remaining three days?

The Public

"Means and Ends: An Inquiry"

Source: Barry D. Cytron.

This activity is a series of classroom lesson plans, with appropriate background material, for stimulating the participants to examine the relationship between means and ends. The philosophical issues raised will be explored by analyzing legal cases. The study begins with background material about the internment of the Japanese Americans during the second World War. (See *The Great Betrayal* by Audrie Girdner and Ann Loftis, Toronto: Macmillan, 1969). Then the students explore the Marco DeFunis case recently argued before the Supreme Court. The ramifications of the DeFunis case have direct bearing on students' lives.

Value concept: Ability to define the differences between means and ends and to identify the ramifications of adhering to one or another consistently (ritual).

Activity: At the conclusion of these lessons, high-school and college students will be able to discern the implications of means and ends in justifying moral and legal attitudes.

Learning aids: Briefs of cases from American legal history, including Korematsu v. United States and De Funis v. Odegaard.

Unit interaction: **1.** Introduce the philosophical concept of means and ends.
2. Explore two cases that center on this value problem.
3. Develop a mock Supreme Court to hear and rule on this issue: Does the end justify the means in pursuit of social equality through affirmative action?

Evaluation: Write an essay prompted by question "Can we better understand capital punishment in light of the means/ends continuum?"

Suggestions: Many cases in American history can be related to this philosophical problem. A reading of other cases will reveal similar moral problems.

"Culture Capsule"

Source: Karen Hockins

Karen, a teacher on a Navajo reservation, outlined this general activity for her class in Arizona. When they completed their capsule of materials, they mailed it to Ames, Iowa. In turn, an Ames classroom had made a capsule, too; and they mailed the Iowa capsule to Karen's class.

Objective: Navajo children will make a capsule containing objects from their culture, which permit others to hear, feel, see, and taste various aspects of the Navajo culture (construction).

Items to be included:

Environment: piece of yucca plant, pinion pine needles, container of sand (for sand-painting), juniper seeds.

Literature: *Kee's Home; Stephanie and the Coyote; Tinker and the Medicine Man; Coyote Tales.*

Music: Tape with Navajo music; type of gourd used as a musical instrument.

Pottery: small wedding vase.

Weaving: small piece of raw wool; piece of wool after carding; piece of wool after spinning; small Navajo saddle blanket.

Foods: bag of pinions; recipe for making fry bread.

Children of both cultures should become aware of similarities and differences between their worlds.

"Freedom"

Source: David Lendt.

Value concept: To encourage members of the class to study their feelings and investigate their values in a situation pitting public interest against personal interest (simulation).

Activity: Role-playing exercise and class discussion.

Learning aids: One role player, in addition to the originator of the exercise (value strategy). The script below.

Unit interaction: A period of approximately seven minutes is allowed for the presentation of the role-playing strategy. Instructions to the class are to listen carefully, to assess major points being made, and to be prepared to discuss the situation.

Evaluation: Ten minutes are allowed for group discussion. In the process, the following questions may be asked to members of the class:

1. Which role do you most identify with?
2. Which player is "right," or is either one right?
3. What principles are involved in the conflict?
4. Given your identification with one of the players, what would you have done differently, if anything?

Role Playing Value Strategy

Role 1: Journalist
Role 2: Teacher in evening adult education course on human sexuality held at local high school.

1: Journalist calls teacher to say he has arranged for a photographer to attend the evening class that evening to take photographs of the members of the class and the teacher.

2: Teacher says he's not sure any such story should be written and certainly no photos should be taken without the approval of the coordinator of adult education.

1: "You are teaching a public course, in a public place, at some public expense. It is therefore open to the public and the press is simply a representative of the public at large. I just want a feature article and feature photo that might be of great interest to many of our readers.

"The press attends council meetings as the eyes and ears of the public, covers fires and other disasters, government, and all sorts of situations and events on behalf of the citizenry. The press can attend school for the citizen as well."

2: "I, too, have some professional prerogatives and I have control of my classroom. I say I don't want you to interfere in my teaching of the course, and that's it."

1: "I respect your right to teach your course as you see fit. All I want is a feature story and photo. I'll come with a photographer either before or after your class session, whenever it's convenient for you and your students.

2: "You don't understand. Many persons in the class are well-known and important people in the community. There are equally important people in town who oppose the use of the schools for sex education, adult or otherwise. Many of those people wouldn't understand. Your appearance here would be an invasion of my students' privacy."

1: "Your students are there of their own free will. They are attending a publicly advertised course in a publicly built plant under a publicly paid teacher. Their privacy is in no way being invaded."

"What are you hiding? I'm suspicious of a public servant who is unwilling to openly discuss or display public affairs in which John Q. Taxpayer—our reader—has a stake. My responsibility is to the public and I smell a rat when bureaucrats begin to balk. Just what's going on in that human sexuality course anyway?"

2: "Nothing that is not wholesome and constructive. It's just that without a proper background, some of the things we do would be difficult to explain to others."

1: "Then background me. I'll be happy to read what you recommend to me. I'll talk at length with you and your students. I'm in no particular hurry. It's just that I'd like the photograph now. I'll have plenty of time for in-depth analysis later."

2: "I just can't buy it. I don't think it will work. I can't risk the good will of my students and my professional reputation on such a story."

1: "I'm out of patience. Whether you like it or not, I intend to be there tonight with my photographer and with my growing curiosity."

2: "I'll cancel the class; we'll meet somewhere else at some other time. You won't be able to find us. Then, what kind of a story would you have?"

1: "Are you kidding?"

"Environmental Questionnaire"

Source: Sue Johannsen.

Value concept: Are our stated ideas about the environment consistent with our actions? (paper-and-pencil test).

Activity: Participants will judge how consistent they are in actions and statements, after filling out two different questionnaires on environmental issues.

Learning aids: Two-part questionnaire.

Unit interaction: Participants are given the first page of the questionnaire and allowed five minutes to complete it. Then they are given an additional five minutes to complete the second part.

Have students rate themselves on how committed they are to a healthier environment, or hold a class discussion about the implications of the two questionnaires.

Evaluation. Self-evaluation.

First questionnaire

1. Do you think we should recycle newspapers and magazines to save our trees?
2. Should Iowa pass a "Ban-the-Can" law similar to Oregon's?
3. Do you believe the world is overpopulated?
4. Have you read about the possible destruction of the ozone layer of our atmosphere by the freon released by spray cans?
5. Do you know the name of a new paper towel and toilet tissue that is made of recycled paper?
6. Do you check soaps and detergents to see if they are biodegradable? Can you name a low phosphate detergent?
7. Would you prefer to see coal mined in an environmentally approved way or conventionally strip-mined?
8. Should the auto industry have been forced to add antipollution devices to cars and go to lead-free gasoline?
8. Would you like to see train travel modernized?
10. Do you think that we will have to conserve fuels in the years ahead or is the "energy crisis" a fake?

Second questionnaire

1. Do you save papers for a collection? Have you ever participated in a recycling effort?
2. Do you buy pop in bottles and return them? (How much are they worth per bottle?)
3. How many nonadopted children do you have or plan to have?
4. Do you buy spray deodorant or roll-on? spray starch or an add to the wash type? paste furniture polish or spray on?
5. Have you ever bought recycled paper products?
6. Have you ever tried a nonphosphate laundry product? Do you use it now?
7. What if reforestation made coal and hence electricity more expensive than it already is? Which method would you then prefer?
8. Have you, or will you, buy a post-1974 car with the antipollution additions? How important is gas mileage to you?
9. Have you taken a train trip recently and left your car at home?
10. Have you, in the last year, cut down on auto trips? Given more thought to whether each one was necessary? Have you checked to see how well-insulated your home is? Have you turned the thermostat down and lights off? Are you trying to save the nation's energy or your own budget?

Other Activities

Chef's delight.   Prepare meals from other countries. Find people in your community who represent various ethnic groups and get recipes from them.

Bumper sticker.   Finds firms which manufacture bumper stickers. They sell blank ones which you can color with magic markers.

Stamps.   Dime stores sell bags of world stamps at low costs. Play detective with them. What clues about the country can you gain from the quality of the engraving, the colors used, the gum, the person or object depicted?

United Nations.   Vary your daily classroom routine with background music from various countries. Write the United Nations. (Source: Jean Gillaspie.)

Short wave radio.   Gain some insights into the feelings and beliefs of people from other lands. Bring a short wave radio to class.

SUMMARY

You have essentially finished this book, and you have just concluded the "easiest" chapter in the book. It was easiest in the sense that I did not have to write most of it. And it seemed easy in another sense, because those teachers who developed the activities were enjoying themselves and getting positive feedback from their classes about the worth of the activities.

Paradoxically, values investment is not easy. This chapter has shown that there is a systematic approach to values education which requires you to make commitments of time and intellectual energy to follow through on value questions.

Please remember, however, that I urged you at the beginning of this book to use it as a way to find out what you personally value and what approach or approaches would make you a more effective values educator. I hope you are able to say now that studying this book has been a good investment. I invite you to share your comments about the book with me.

As I look at the future of the values education movement, I wonder if it will continue to grow as dramatically as it has in the past decade. As a historian, I think that it might diminish in a few years. Yet I hope that it will not decline because, if values educators take more seriously the need to assess value positions, and can in fact demonstrate that values education does make a difference, then the future will be brighter.

All of us owe our gratitude to many past values educators. May their investment in us bring a worthy return. I hope that you will be able in the future to act more creatively upon your values.

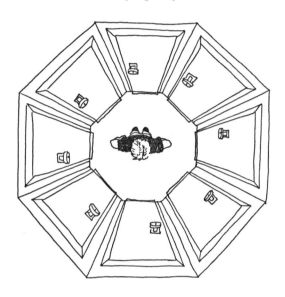

Notes

1. Martin N. Olson, "Ways to Achieve Quality in School Classrooms: Some Definite Answers," *Phi Delta Kappan* 53, no. 1 (September 1971): 63–65.

2. Catherine Landreth, *Early Childhood Behavior and Learning* (New York: Random House, 1967), pp. 284–324, 352–66; Lester and Alice Crow, *Child Development and Adjustment* (New York: Macmillan, 1962), pp. 323–72, 390–422.

3. Gisela Konopka, *Young Girls: A Portrait of Adolescence* (Englewood Cliffs, N.J.: Prentice-Hall, 1976). Konopka heads the Center for Youth Development and Research, University of Minnesota. In her interviews with youths, she finds that most young adults and teenagers have sound relationships with their parents, contrary to idea of the "generation gap."

4. Philip Aries, *Centuries of Childhood* (New York: Knopf, 1962). The *History of Education Quarterly*, among other scholarly publications, offers occasional articles on the historical perspectives adults have had about children.

5. See, for example, *Search for Meaning*, Pflaum/Standard, as described in Chapter 3.

6. The Coronada, California, school district has developed its own units of instruction on the power of advertising. Douglas Superka, et al., *Values Education Sourcebook* (Boulder, Col.: Social Science Education Consortium, 1976) describes their program. Sev-

eral environmental agencies have produced materials relating to use of leisure and recreational time. For texts in this field, read Howard G. Danford, revised by Max Shirley, *Creative Leadership in Recreation* (Boston: Allyn & Bacon, 1970); and James F. Murphy, *Recreation and Leisure Service: A Humanistic Perspective* (Dubuque, Iowa: Brown, 1975).

7. Virginia Satir, *Conjoint Family Therapy* (Science and Behavior Books, 1964).

8. Louis Phillips, "Humor in the Classroom," *Learning* **2**, no. 8 (April 1974): 74–78.

A

Related Readings

GENERAL REFERENCES

Bellanca, James D. *Values and the Search for Self*. Washington, D.C.: National Education Association, 1975.

Chazan, Barry I., and Soltis, Jonas F., eds. *Moral Education*. New York: Teachers College Press, 1972.

Inlow, Gail M. *Values in Transition: A Handbook*. New York: Wiley, 1972.

Lyon, Harold. *Learning to Feel—Feeling to Learn: Humanistic Education for the Whole Man*. Columbus, Ohio: Merrill, 1971.

Patterson, C. H. *Humanistic Education*. Englewood Cliffs, N.J.: Prentice-Hall, 1973.

Phenix, Philip H. *Education and the Worship of God*. Philadelphia: Westminster, 1966.

Phi Delta Kappa. *Values in American Education*. Bloomington, Ind.: Phi Delta Kappa, 1964.

DESCRIPTIONS OF SCHOOLING TODAY

Cullum, Albert. *The Geranium on the Window Sill Just Died But Teacher You Went Right On*. New York: Harlin Quist, 1971.

Silberman, Charles. *Crisis in the Classroom.* New York: Random House, 1970.

Smith, L. Glenn, and Kniker, Charles R. *Myth and Reality.* 2nd ed. Boston: Allyn & Bacon, 1975.

HISTORY OF EDUCATION

Katz, Michael B., ed. *Education in American History.* New York: Praeger, 1973.

Lannie, Vincent. "The Teaching of Values in Public, Sunday and Catholic Schools: An Historical Perspective," *Religious Education* 70, no. 2 (March-April 1975): 115–37.

McCluskey, Neil G. *Public Schools and Moral Education.* New York: Columbia University Press, 1958.

PHILOSOPHY OF EDUCATION/TEACHER MODELS

Bricker, D.C. "Moral Education and Teacher Neutrality," *School Review* 80, no. 4 (1972): 619–27.

Broudy, Harry S., and Palmer, John R. *Exemplars of Teaching Method.* Chicago: Rand McNally, 1965.

Carter, J. E. "Trends in the Teaching of Values," *Contemporary Education* 44, no. 5 (April 1973): 295–97.

Crabtree, Walden. "Establishing Policy in the Values Education Controversy," *Contemporary Education* 46, no. 1 (February 1974): 24–27.

Fraenkel, Jack R. "Strategies for Developing Values," *Today's Education* 63, no. 7 (November-December 1974): 49–55.

Jackson, Philip W. *Life in Classrooms.* New York: Holt, 1968.

Jarrett, James L. *The Humanities and Humanistic Education.* Reading, Mass.: Blaisdell, 1973.

Kachaturoff, G. "Teaching Values in Public Schools: Ethical and Moral Values," *The Social Studies* 64, no. 6 (October 1973): 222–26.

Willower, D. J. "Schools, Values and Educational Inquiry," *Educational Administration Quarterly* 9, no. 2 (Spring 1973): 1–18.

VALUE THEORIES

Albert, E. M., and Kluckhohn, Clyde. *A Selected Bibliography on Values, Ethics, and Aesthetics.* New York: Free Press, 1959.

Baier, K., and Rescher, Nicholas. *Values and the Future.* New York: Macmillan, 1969.

Bull, Norman J. *Moral Judgement from Childhood to Adolescence.* Beverly Hills, Calif.: Sage, 1970.

Laszlo, E., and Wilbur, J. B. *Value Theory in Philosophy and Social Science.* New York: Gorden and Breach, 1973.

Lorr, Maurice. "The Structure of Values, Conceptions of the Desirable," *Journal of Research in Personality* 7, no. 2 (September 1973): 137–47.

Margolis, J. *Values and Conduct.* New York: Oxford University Press, 1971.

Peters, Richard S. *Ethics and Education.* London: George Allen and Unwin, 1966.

Progressive Education, **27,** no. 6 (April 1950). (The entire issue is devoted to questions about values education.)

Strommen, Merton P., ed. *Research on Religious Development.* New York: Hawthorn, 1971, especially the essay by Martin L. Hoffman, "Development of Internal Moral Standards in Children," pp. 211–63.

Wilson, John, et al. *Introduction to Moral Education.* Baltimore: Penguin, 1968.

CURRICULUM AND PROGRAMMING

Alpren, Morton M. "Curriculum Theory of the Affective Domain," *Theory into Practice* **13,** no. 1 (February 1974): 46–53.

Borton, Terry. *Reach, Touch and Teach.* New York: McGraw-Hill, 1970.

Dunfee, Maxine, and Crump, Claudia. *Teaching for Social Values in Social Studies.* Washington, D.C.: Association for Childhood Education International, 1974.

Fagen, Stanley A., and Checkon, Stephen. *Issues in Measuring Teacher Competence for Affective Education* (April 1972), ED 065 554.

Flynn, Elizabeth W., and LaFaso, John F. *Designs in Affective Education.* New York: Paulist Press, 1974.

Hall, Brian P. *Value Clarification as Learning Process: A Guidebook of Learning Strategies.* New York: Paulist Press, 1973.

Hendricks, Gay, and Fadiman, James. *Transpersonal Education: A Curriculum of Affect and Being.* Englewood Cliffs, N.J.: Prentice-Hall, 1976.

Jensen, Larry. *What's Right, What's Wrong.* Washington, D.C.: Public Affairs Press, 1975.

Johnson, David and Johnson, Roger. *Learning Together and Alone.* Englewood Cliffs, N.J.: Prentice-Hall, 1975.

Valett, Robert E. *Affective-Humanistic Education.* Belmont, Calif.: Lear Siegler, 1974.

B

Addresses of Publishers and Suppliers

Abbey Press
St. Meinrad,
Ind. 47577

ACI Films, Inc.
35 W. 45th St.
New York, N.Y. 10036

Achievement Motivation Program
111 E. Wacker Drive
Suite 510
Chicago, Ill. 60601

Association for Instructional Materials (AIM)
600 Madison Ave.
New York, N.Y. 10022

Argus Communications
7440 Natchez Ave.
Niles, Ill. 60648

Augsburg Publishing House
426 S. 5th St.
Minneapolis, Minn. 55415

Bailey Film Associates
2211 Michigan Ave.
Santa Monica, Calif. 90404

Big Sur Recordings
Box 4119
San Rafael, Calif. 94903

BFA Educational Media
Santa Monica, Calif. 71001

R. R. Bowker Company
1180 Avenue of the Americas
New York, N.Y. 19936

Carousel Films
1501 Broadway
New York, N.Y. 10036

CCM Films, Inc.
866 Third Ave.
New York, N.Y. 10022

Center Cinema Co-op
237 E. Ontario
Chicago, Ill. 60611

Center for Cassette Studies
8110 Webb Ave
North Hollywood, Calif. 91605

The Center for Humanities, Inc.
Two Holland Ave.
White Plains, N.Y. 10603

Churchill Films
662 N. Robotson Blvd.
Los Angeles, Calif. 90069

Creative Film Society
14558 Valero St.
Van Nuys, Calif. 91405

Disseminators of Knowledge
71 Radcliffe Road
Buffalo, N.Y. 14214

Ealing Company
2225 Massachusetts Ave.
Cambridge, Mass. 02140

Eastman Kodak Company
Rochester, N.Y. 14650

Economics Press, Inc.
12 Daniel Road
Fairfield, N.J. 07006

Encyclopedia Britannica Educational Corp. (EBEC)
425 N. Michigan Ave.
Chicago, Ill. 60611

Eye Gate
146-01 Archer Ave.
Jamaica, N.Y. 11435

Fearon Publishers
6 Davis Drive
Belmont, Calif. 94002

Fides Publishers, Inc.
Notre Dame, Ind. 46556

Film Distributors International
2221 S. Olive St.
Los Angeles, Calif. 90007

Films Incorporated
4420 Oakton St.
Skokie, Ill. 60076

Friendship Press
P.O. Box 37844
Cincinnati, Ohio 45237

Guidance Associates
Pleasantville, N.Y. 10570

Indiana University
Audio-Visual Center
Bloomington, Ind. 47401

Interact
Box 202
Lakeside, Calif. 92040

International Film Bureau, Inc.
332 S. Michigan Ave.
Chicago, Ill. 60604

Learning Corporation of America
711 Fifth Ave.
New York, N.Y. 10022

Learning Magazine
c/o Education Today Company, Inc.
530 University Ave.
Palo Alto, Calif. 94301

Mass Media Ministries
2116 N. Charles St.
Baltimore, Md. 21218

McGraw-Hill/Contemporary Films
Princeton Road
Heightstown, N.J. 08520

National Audio-Visual Center
General Services Administration
Washington, D.C. 20409

New York Times
229 W. 43rd St.
New York, N.Y. 10036

Parents Magazine Films, Inc.
52 Vanderbilt Ave.
New York, N.Y. 10017

Pathescope
71 Weyman Ave.
New Rochelle, N.Y. 10802

Paulist Productions
P.O. Box 1057
Pacific Palisades, Calif. 90272

Pennant Educational Materials
4680 Alvaredo Canyon Road
San Diego, Calif. 92120

Pflaum/Standard
38 W. Fifth St.
Dayton, Ohio 45402

Psychology Today
Box 2990
Boulder, Colo. 80302

Pyramid Films
Box 1048
Santa Monica, Calif. 90406

Sage Publications, Inc.
P. O. Box 776
Beverly Hills, Calif. 90210

Sandak, Inc.
180 Harvard Ave.
Stamford, Conn. 06902

Schloat Productions
150 White Plains Road
Tarrytown, N.Y. 10591

Serina Press
70 Kennedy St.
Alexandria, Va. 22305

Society for Visual Education
1345 Diversey Pkwy.
Chicago, Ill. 60614

Steck-Vaughn
P. O. Box 2028
Austin, Tex. 78767

Universal Education and Visual Arts
221 Park Ave. South
New York, N.Y. 10003

Western Behavioral Sciences Institute
1150 Silverado
La Jolla, Calif. 92037

Winston Press
25 Groveland Terrace
Minneapolis, Minn. 55403

Indexes

Subject Index

Name Index

Activities Index